The Smoker's H

James Sc

Thorsons

An Imprint of HarperCollins*Publishers*

Thorsons
An Imprint of HarperCollins*Publishers*
77–85 Fulham Palace Road,
Hammersmith, London W6 8JB

Published by Thorsons 1993
1 3 5 7 9 10 8 6 4 2

A catalogue record for this book
is available from the British Library

ISBN 0 7225 2922 8

Phototypeset by Harper Phototypesetters Limited,
Northampton, England
Printed in Great Britain by
HarperCollinsManufacturing Glasgow

Contents

Preface

Some people can stop smoking, and I hope they do. Others never will. Just as I'd like all overweight people to slim and those with high blood pressure to diet and alcoholics to stop drinking, I would call on smokers to give up – but I know life's not like that.

Around 1,631,540 cigarettes are lit every minute. Smoking has such positive associations for so many people, that they will always smoke. It follows that many other people will live and work with smokers. I believe that people CAN minimise the effects of smoking, tobacco use, and breathing bad air – and this book is the result.

Even though my primary audience is those who won't stop smoking, people who do manage to stop will still benefit from following its teachings because the effects of the habit linger. Others can take advantage of it too – people who love smokers and think that living with them is worth the extra health risk of passive smoking, and children who live in a smoking house-hold and have no choice. This book is for smokers and anyone who lives, works or spends time with a smoker.

The book can also help a wider range of people – anyone forced to breathe less than pure air. That includes people who live and work in cities, or work around smoke, solvents and chemicals and suffer similar health problems to smokers. Despite the difficulties of their environment, they can still gain a longer, healthier life.

Although the main focus is on smoking, my words also apply to tobacco chewers. They are at risk from the various forms of mouth cancer, including tongue, oesophagus, cheek and gum cancer. I believe that their risk of mouth cancer is higher than smokers' risk of lung cancer compared with non-smokers'.

A special word about children. Children have no choice – if a parent smokes, they smoke. If a mother smokes during pregnancy, the baby smokes. Similarly, children who live in cities effectively smoke because of the pollution all around them. So the plans and advice in this book are for them as well. Children will benefit from my teachings more than their parents because they will start earlier with a healthy lifestyle and thus have an even better chance of a disease-free life.

Why Do People Smoke?

Tobacco smoke contains about 900 clearly identifiable chemical components. Some produce feelings of intoxication similar to alcohol, others can even be hallucinogenic. It's easy to imagine how the first smokers – native Indians of Central and South

America – burned tobacco, inhaled the smoke and felt the pleasant effects of the experience. Gradually they learned to use tobacco leaves selectively to enhance the pleasure.

Shamans – ancient medicine men or priests – believed tobacco helped create a good relationship with the gods they worshipped. Consequently, they encouraged its use and helped foster the cultivation and curing of tobacco. Cigars and cigarettes as we know them were comparatively modern, largely European inventions. Smoking through special tubes and pipes was the original method of inhalation. As well as being smoked, tobacco was chewed, infused for use as beverages and its dried dust was sniffed.

In his log of 1492, Columbus wrote about one of the native Indian practices: 'They packed a tube called a tabac with an herb, lit one end, and drank smoke from the other end.' Columbus saw no practical value to 'drinking' smoke and said no more. In dismissing the smoking habit, he misjudged the human tendency to enjoy tobacco that was to become an enormous, world-wide industry.

Among the Mayan Indians, tobacco was used so extensively that primitive syringes were developed to administer tobacco enemas, which enabled its chemicals to be absorbed rapidly into the bloodstream. There is no doubt that people could get 'high' from tobacco used in these ingenious and dangerous ways, which probably also caused serious illness and even death. Nicotine is highly toxic in concentration – a strong enough infusion can kill most insects and a single drop of pure nicotine on a rabbit's skin is enough to kill the animal. Primitive ways of using tobacco were bound to have produced overdoses.

Tobacco use is probably over 8,000 years old, but reactions to it have varied over the centuries. Tobacco has been both encouraged and outlawed. In the early 20th century it was widely accepted. Until the late 1950s some doctors considered it healthy and even recommended it to 'melancholic' patients. During the blitz bombings of the Second World War a cigarette was always at hand for air raid victims.

Because smoking was viewed as a pleasure, tobacco has been taxed in most countries since about the 16th century. But advances in medical science meant that by the 1980s the mood had changed. It began to be seen as bad for your health and looked upon as a vice, while non-smokers decided that it was positively offensive.

Much research has been devoted to trying to understand what benefits are gained by using tobacco. Some common reasons people have given are:

- 'I can concentrate better when I'm smoking.'
- 'I can cope with stress if I'm able to smoke.'
- 'Smoking calms me down. I feel relaxed and able to accept things.'
- 'Smoking lifts my spirits. I feel more cheerful.'

The Ill Effects

Findings seem to confirm that smoking helps depressed personalities, but we also know that it is highly addictive. It is, simply, very difficult for people to stop smoking. Withdrawal symptoms are similar to those of any other addictive drug. They include tension, restlessness, irritability, increased hunger, inability to concentrate and insomnia. All of them are relieved by giving the smoker more nicotine, confirming that it is the addictive component. Not only humans are subject to nicotine addiction. It can happen to primates too, and indeed monkeys chew tobacco quite naturally, learn to smoke easily, and suffer the same withdrawal symptoms.

Smoking's major ill effects – heart disease, stroke and cancer – should however be separated from its addictive qualities. While nicotine is the addictive substance in tobacco, life-threatening illnesses are usually the result of other components. Nicotine may however be implicated in high blood pressure. Most importantly, tobacco smoke is not filtered by our digestive processes like other potentially toxic chemicals such as caffeine. So tobacco's toxins are pulled directly into the lungs which facilitate their movement into the bloodstream.

Tobacco Toxicity

Scientists have now developed an index of toxicity according to how much of a substance is required to kill rats and mice: the LD-50 test. The level necessary to kill 50 per cent of the animals is called the substance's LD-50. Nicotine has an LD-50 of 0.3 milligrams per kilogram if injected intravenously, or 9.5 milligrams if simply injected into a body cavity such as the abdomen. In practical terms, to kill someone who weighs 70 kg (11 stone), it would be necessary to inject only 21 milligrams of nicotine into a vein or 665 milligrams into the abdominal cavity. So about one teaspoonful of nicotine would be enough to kill seven people.

Tobacco grown for commercial purposes contains about eight per cent nicotine. You would therefore only have to chew about ten grams of tobacco in order to get enough nicotine to be highly toxic or even lethal. The lower levels we get from smoking it do their own harm in their own time.

CHAPTER ONE

A Calculated Risk –
Minimising the Consequences
of Smoking

Tobacco use has risks like many other things we choose to do. But because the health risks associated with smoking receive so much publicity, everyone simply tells smokers to stop. As we know, this is not as easy as it sounds. No one seems to ask, 'Could there be a compromise? Is there something the smoker can do to reduce the risks while still smoking?' Smoking does indeed carry risks, but they CAN be reduced – and this book shows you how.

The risks of smoking are so unique and well defined that smokers pay higher life insurance premiums than non-smokers. Most smokers are aware of smoking's health risks, but they accept them without giving them much thought. If they just stopped to consider how to offset the risks, it would be possible to minimise the health compromise that smoking entails.

Lung cancer is a case in point. Original smoking studies in the US and the UK showed that the risk of cancer was proportionate to the number of cigarettes smoked and their tar content. These studies also showed that the rate of lung cancer among some people who smoked was just slightly higher than for those who didn't smoke. Why? The answer is simple. Those smokers who didn't get cancer, on average, ate foods rich in antioxidants which can dramatically reduce the risk of cancer, heart disease and other less spectacular illnesses such as cataracts. In addition, these people's diets included three other protective substances: the B vitamins, vitamin E, and vitamin C.

Japanese smokers have about half the lung cancer rate of American and British smokers in spite of the fact that Japanese cigarettes are stronger and have more tar, and most Japanese smoke for longer than other smokers. Based on these facts, you would expect the Japanese lung cancer rate to be higher than elsewhere. In fact, their lower lung cancer rates show that smoking does not automatically result in the disease. Again, dietary differences provide the explanation. The Japanese diet is rich in protective antioxidant foods and the green tea which they use widely has a special, preventative effect.

When smoking seemed to be a positive risk factor influencing the development of lung cancer, scientists and doctors took the easy approach and advised 'Stop smoking'. But by taking this narrow view, no-one bothered to spell out the other side of the story: that by following a good diet, taking the correct supplements and exercising, the risk of lung cancer can be reduced.

Many more subtle variations in lifestyle also have to be taken into account. For example, apart from obvious ethnic and genetic differences, factors such as the consumption of vegetables, fruit, meat and fish, how much you drink and the amount of exercise you take are all relevant. So does whether you live in a crowded city, drive regularly in heavy traffic, or work with chemicals – all of which can predispose you towards lung cancer. The risk factor associated with smoking also varies depending on how many cigarettes you smoke, the types of tobacco, the filters and types of filters. Chewing tobacco is a serious risk with its own variations such as the amount chewed, the method of chewing, additives in the tobacco and so on.

Thus even a clear-cut risk is not as clearly defined as we're often led to believe. Similarly, it is not clear precisely how much of the risk-reducing factors are required in order to produce a protective effect. One definite result of studies has shown that eating vegetables decreases cancer risks in smokers. But this finding poses more questions: Which vegetables? More vegetables in general, or selected vegetables? Is there a relationship between the number of cigarettes and the servings of vegetables? Is fruit as good? There is simply no end to this kind of question. Nailing down the details could keep research scientists busy for decades.

In general, epidemiologists – scientists who study health and environmental conditions – keep confirming what we know: smoking, living with a smoker, working in a city with poor air, increases your health risks. However, many of these health risks also increase with age and poor diet. You could live in the most idyllic Garden of Eden, and still run the risk of developing cancer, heart disease, cataracts to name but a few as you got older. 'That's life,' as they say. But smoking does accelerate all these possibilities, especially the 'diseases of aging', and makes them worse. By correcting your lifestyle habits, you can reduce the rate at which these risks accumulate. Some susceptibilities, such as cataracts, can be reduced to less than that of non-smokers with an otherwise unhealthy lifestyle.

TABLE 1.1 *Tobacco use risks that can be reduced by diet and lifestyle changes*

Cosmetic	Cancer	Diseases of Aging
Age spots	Aerodigestive	Asthma
Eye clarity	(mouth,	Cataracts
Gum tone	oesophagus,	Emphysema
Hair sheen	etc.)	Heart disease
Poor fingernails	Bladder	Hypertension
Skin colour	Colonic	Nasal polyps
Skin wrinkles	Leukaemia	Osteoporosis
	Lung	Periodontal disease
	Pancreatic	Ulcers
	Rectal	

Most of these risks result from oxidative toxins in smoke which cause cellular damage, plus the metabolic effects of smoking and its general irritating effects on the body systems. These can all be reduced considerably by taking the appropriate measures outlined in this book and following a lifestyle that gives you a good chance of normal health.

Table 1.2 shows the problems that can be reduced by

selecting foods and food supplements specifically rich in antioxidants.

TABLE 1.2 *Risks related to insufficient antioxidants*

Cosmetic	Cancer	Aging
Age spots	Aerodigestive	Cataracts
Skin colour	Bladder	Emphysema
Skin wrinkles	Colon and rectal	Heart disease
	Lung	Hypertension
	Pancreatic	

Smokers and Diet

Only around nine per cent of people eat enough fruit and vegetables daily, so you can see that smokers aren't alone in failing to follow a balanced and varied diet. But they do have a reputation for being a little worse than average, although their smoking habit dictates that they should be better than average.

Research published in such prestigious medical journals as the *American Journal of Clinical Nutrition* and the *American Journal of Public Health*, among others, have reported the following:

- Smokers eat too much meat
- Smokers don't eat as much fruit and vegetables as non-smokers.
- Smokers don't eat as much cereal as non-smokers.
- Smokers are likely to consume more coffee and alcohol than non-smokers.

- Smokers are likely to be short of vitamins A, C, E, folic acid, several other B-vitamins and the minerals calcium, selenium and zinc.

In fact smokers need MORE nutrients, especially antioxidants and antioxidant nutrients such as vitamins E and C, than average people. Diet surveys prove they are getting LESS. They definitely need more fibre than other people, yet they eat less. The evidence suggests that they should limit tea and coffee drinking, and choose fruit or vegetable juices or herbal teas, but they seem to do the opposite.

I have already mentioned Japanese smokers, and how they have a lower incidence of lung cancer than most American and British people. But they also have a lower incidence of everything on Table 1.1. When all differences between Japanese and other smokers are considered, it comes down to diet, because other Japanese lifestyle habits, such as exercise, are even worse than in the West. But their low-fat, more vegetarian diet is better than ours by a long stretch.

In Britain and the United States, smokers' diets contribute significantly to their risk. Look back to Table 1.1. Certain illnesses such as various cancers, cataracts, and hypertension are more related to diet than to smoking. And we do know from the many studies of smokers that they don't select their food well. If that's not bad enough, only a small percentage of adults use a daily food supplement whether they smoke or not. All smokers need supplements regularly – taking them occasionally isn't enough! Smokers need above-average levels of all nutrients, and significantly more of the B vitamins and antioxidant nutrients which include vitamins C, E and beta carotene. They can also get additional protective benefits from other selected vegetables, additional fibre and fish rich in the right oils.

These nutritional shortfalls, as I call them, aren't great enough for you to notice them or for your doctor to diagnose them as a deficiency. But they do accumulate over the years. This is one reason why women who smoke are more likely to develop osteoporosis. It also explains why smoking accelerates the onset of cataracts and why bladder cancer is more likely among smokers. Eating correctly need not cost more and can pay excellent dividends for everyone – especially smokers.

When to Start Your Anti-Risk Diet

Start now! I'm often asked, 'I've been smoking for over 20 years, so what's the point of starting a new health programme now?' My answer is always the same: 'Time after time, research has conclusively proven that your body can improve at any age. Since this is the first moment of the rest of your life, NOW is the best time to start. It doesn't matter if you're 19 or 90 years of age. Start now!'

I've already mentioned a few ways to reduce risks and explained that, as a smoker, you are less likely to eat fruits and vegetables than non-smokers, even though you need more. I also said smokers need more nutrients. I want to start you off on this track by asking you to do two simple things:

- Drink two glasses of fresh unsweetened orange juice a day, or eat two oranges or two kiwi fruit.
- Eat some red fruits and vegetables every day: for example, a tomato salad, red pepper, watermelon, or all of them.

CHAPTER TWO

Oxidation – the Toxic Trap

Life depends on oxygen in the air. We see oxygen's interaction with other substances – the process of oxidation – whenever we strike a match, start our car or notice rusty metal. The same kind of process takes place in our body, at body temperature and faster than a match can flare or a car engine burst into life. And, if we worked at the snail's pace of rust, we wouldn't survive at all.

Oxidation is fuelled by similar chemicals, whether they are in your car's engine or your stomach. Fats are chemically very like petrol, and carbohydrates, which are already partially oxidised in the plant that makes them, differ only slightly. How does the same process that can occur at body temperature also take place at great heat in a car engine, and how does it happen so fast in our body compared to the slow rate of rust?

The instant you breathe in, your blood traps oxygen with iron and transports it to all the body tissues, where it's passed on to your body's 50 trillion cells. In these cells the oxygen combines with carbon and hydrogen. The oxygen-carbon mix makes carbon dioxide. The hydrogen passed to oxygen produces water. Both chemical actions release energy by burning just as the car engine does. As soon as you breathe out, you release the wastes – carbon dioxide and water. You can't see the carbon dioxide, but on a cold day you can see the water, as vapour, when you exhale.

Our body performs this intricate series of chemical reactions through the elaborate process of metabolism. Metabolism is effected by means of enzymes – natural catalysts which lower the energy barriers like the spark plug in a car or the friction of striking a match. Many enzymes work to make oxidation occur at body temperature, not at the hundreds of degrees required by man-made processes. The remarkable human body is able to extract more energy from a pound of fuel than even the most advanced man-made engines. Not only does nature perform the same processes at body temperature, but it is more efficient as well!

It isn't surprising that your body is more efficient than a car engine. It represents over four billion years of life that has been developing on earth, and most forms of life have been using oxygen for over two billion of those years. That's a lot of time for nature to test many options and decide which ones work well.

But what about that rusty nail? Rust is a natural process, yet it is unwanted and illustrates that some forms of oxidation are not wanted. Other common forms of oxidation that we don't necessarily want are cooking oils going rancid, opened wine going vinegary, and apples turning brown.

The simplest way to prevent oxidation is to shut out

oxygen. For example, we put an airtight stopper in a wine bottle or a screw top on a jar of oil. We paint cars and galvanise nails. We can also slow the oxidation process by refrigerating oils and even freezing foods. Alternatively, we can introduce a material that reacts with the oxygen more easily than the thing we want to protect. For instance, squeezing lemon juice on a cut apple makes chemicals in the lemon juice react with the oxygen in the air and keeps the oxygen from attacking the apple itself until the lemon juice has been used up. A material that reacts easily with oxygen in order to protect something else is called an antioxidant.

In our environment, many things can cause unwanted oxidation. All living things must in fact resist oxidising agents in order to survive. Our body depends on a complex system of antioxidants to protect itself, just as we protect metal, cooking oil and food. Natural barriers such as skin, saliva and tears provide a primary defence to keep oxidative materials out of our bodies. However, many oxidants get past the barriers, so nature's secondary strategy is to sacrifice other materials – internal antioxidants – to neutralise oxidative reactions.

Oxygen is the main chemical which causes oxidation, but there are many others, such as nitrates, carbon monoxide, chlorinated hydrocarbons, superoxides and so on. In any oxidation process, atoms are shifted from one material to another. This is done by shifting their electrons in much the same way as electrons flow in the electrical wiring of your home to make lamps light. When desirable electron transfers take place, the process is carefully controlled and the atoms are not released until the process is complete. This is because there is an intermediate stage when the oxidising agent (usually oxygen) has an electron that isn't attached correctly. This atom with the extra electron is known as a radical. So oxidative processes in the body use oxygen radicals as an important step in energy production.

When unwanted oxidation occurs, a similar radical is produced, but it's not well ordered and tightly held within the living cell. You can think of it as 'loose' and looking for attachment at any cost. This loose – or free – radical does not have a planned and organised place in the system. It can combine with an important material, and do irreparable damage. We say a free radical is highly reactive, because nature must combine it with something very quickly in order to maintain harmony.

Free radicals – these intermediate stages of oxidation – are so reactive that scientists speak about their lifetimes in terms of nanoseconds, or millionths of a second. They react more quickly than the most powerful explosive, even though they are the size of atoms. You can think of them as super-explosives that can destroy small, essential parts of a living system. These reactions take place at molecular level, so we can't even watch them with the most powerful microscope. All we can do is assess the accumulated damage of their reactions later on when they show up as health defects.

Free radicals react most easily with fatty chemicals that form the membranes of cells. These fatty materials often have 'unsaturated' regions which are full of electrons. Because the free radical is usually one electron short, it reacts with those materials that have an abundance of electrons. Once this reaction occurs, new unwanted chemicals are produced and the normally well-organised cell membrane develops a flaw. This flaw is a break in nature's first line of defence.

Other natural processes, such as radiation, produce free radicals directly. For example, visible light produces some free radicals that are essential for photosynthesis, the basis of all food. But the ultraviolet light (UV) part of the light spectrum produces unwanted free radicals, so plants must have antioxidants whose major role is to neutralise them. Some of these such as beta carotene are essential to protect the process of photosynthesis. Others, such as ascorbic acid (vitamin C) protect fruit from damage, and vitamin E protects the oils in nuts and seeds. In fact nature has made a wise choice in this strategy of neutralising free radicals, because just about every unwanted oxidative reaction must pass through this intermediate stage.

Also, all free radicals need to neutralise their electrons. By placing free radical neutralisers – the antioxidants – in specific locations, one natural strategy can stop all unwanted oxidative processes. This strategy calls for many antioxidants, and thankfully they are plentiful in nature. Humans depend on many of the antioxidants provided by plants. Indeed some foods such as carrots, cabbage and pumpkins probably owe their widespread cultivation to unconscious human demand for antioxidants long before the days of science.

Over the years scientists have called antioxidants by many different names. 'Free radical scavenger' and 'natural reducing agents' were popular at one time. The simple 'antioxidant' has caught on recently and is used widely.

Free Radical Damage

What does all this mean to smokers? Certain substances have a particular ability to generate free radicals. Tobacco smoke is one of them. Others are fats, and heavy metals. A body that is already under stress from smoking will be more prone to producing free radicals and creating a destructive chain reaction.

In the human body, free radicals react with biochemicals that are essential to the life processes. These essential materials can be circulating in our blood, holding tissues together, components of living cells, even the genetic material that allows a cell to reproduce and build new tissue or produce a child. The damage that may be done is both important and insidious.

When a free radical interacts with something in our blood or any body fluid, it can produce a foreign material that may be poisonous: a toxin. If a cancer-causing toxin is produced, we can expect big trouble later on.

Once a toxin is produced our body must get rid of it if at all possible. Getting rid of the toxin means passing it through our excretory system, including the intestinal tract, kidneys and bladder. If we continue to produce the toxin, we increase the chances of overwhelming our other defences and the chances of it causing effects such as cancer or high blood pressure will increase. So the longer we expose ourselves to a free radical without neutralising it or the toxins it can produce, the greater our risk.

Another frequent site of attack might be an essential component of the delicate cell membrane. If this membrane is compromised, it can allow essential cell materials to leak out or toxic materials to leak in. You can think of it as a break in the insulation of an electric wire, a minute break in a gas pipe or a tiny hole in a gas balloon. Any one of these situations might go unnoticed for a time, but if uncorrected could have disastrous consequences later on. Worse, if it continues, its effects could accumulate and cause an entire system to break down.

Suppose the attack occurs in a place where the by-products of the free radical and antioxidant can't be removed – such as the lens of your eye or the wall of a heart artery. In either case, you will have a damaged site that can get larger. The damage develops a life of its own and grows almost like a cancer. In fact, that's how heart disease develops. A damaged site in a blood vessel is covered and smoothed with fatty material, called cholesterol or plaque, and it continues to grow.

By-products of free radical attack go unnoticed when they first occur because they are so small. Your body consists of 50 trillion cells – if one is damaged, you'd never know. In addition, each cell is composed of billions of atoms arranged in complex chemical structures. If one is destroyed, you'd never feel it. However, if the damage goes unrepaired or continues to take place regularly, eventually it will accumulate and be noticed. Once the damage is obvious, it is usually too late to correct. That's why we say a free radical attack is insidious – you don't know it's taking place until it has reached a high level.

Now let's look at how specific smoking damage can work. Suppose a combination of oxygen and nitrogen from cigarette smoke has a free radical reaction with something in our blood, and the nitrous oxide is converted to a nitrosamine that causes cancer. Suppose another free radical upsets the delicate oil balance in one of our cell membranes, allowing the nitrosamine to enter the cell. That cell is set up to become cancerous. You wouldn't notice for a while, but let it reproduce every week or so for 20 years, and you would have a sizable cancerous tumour.

Suppose the free radicals from carbon monoxide in cigarettes (or polluted air) react with a cell lining the wall of one of our heart arteries. The body responds by covering it with smooth, waxy cholesterol, so the blood still flows smoothly. This is the beginning of the sludge on an artery wall that causes heart disease. As the process continues, the sludge continues to build up. By defending itself with cholesterol, the body sows seeds of its own destruction. It's a short-term solution that has disastrous consequences. Cholesterol protects the artery in the short term, but as it continues to build, eventually clogs it.

Or suppose free radical damage occurs to one cell in the lens of your eye. Although it can't be seen, this single cell forms a damaged spot that scatters light and helps other free radicals form in the cells around it. You can't see the cataract until enough of these reactions have occurred. Once cataracts are established, the only solution is to operate and replace the eye lens. This operation is now routine and usually restores vision completely. However, prevention is still the best medicine.

Each of these examples is important because it shows how tiny, cellular changes can often lead to serious and even life-threatening diseases. Each is insidious because it occurs at such a microscopic level and so slowly that it can't be seen or felt – not even for decades! Who needs to die early or put up with the discomfort of surgery?

Antioxidants to the Rescue

Nature has developed many ways to deal with free radicals and oxidising agents. Let's look at the systems we humans have available for keeping the oxidising agents in cigarette smoke out of our bodies, and for neutralising them.

We are still in the process of discovering antioxidants. We've learned that some nutrients, like vitamins C and E, have a dual role in life. They are essential in the chemical processes that make up metabolism, and they are also effective as antioxidants. Scientists have established the Recommended Nutritional Intake (RNI) of nutrients the body needs. These amounts are usually very small. But the body needs much higher amounts of nutrients if they are to act as antioxidants.

If an antioxidant is also a vitamin, it must serve two masters. As an antioxidant, it is sacrificed when it neutralises an oxidising agent. But as a vitamin in the metabolism, it gets used over and over again. Therefore, when we find antioxidants that also protect vitamins, they have an even greater potential for doing good. If antioxidants are 'protectors', then antioxidant vitamins are 'protector vitamins'. Vitamin C is an excellent example of the latter.

Antioxidants can occur in unexpected places. Our eyes are bathed with a fluid we call tears. Tears continually flush our eyes to remove irritants, such as smoke and fumes. But tears are active. They contain materials which kill germs and antioxidants to neutralise some oxidising agents. There are antioxidants inside the eyes as well. That's why, on a windy day or in irritating fumes, our eyes produce tears profusely.

Similarly, all mucous membranes including the lungs are bathed by fluids that offer two forms of protection. These fluids – alveolar fluid in the lungs, mucus in the nasal passages, saliva in the mouth – trap unwanted materials so they can be eliminated. Second, these fluids contain antioxidants that neutralise some of the oxidising agents. Smoke and fumes have the immediate effect of causing the nasal passages to produce more fluid to counteract them and to neutralise the toxins they contain. This is one reason why smokers often cough and blow their noses often.

In addition to fluids, our nasal passages are lined with minute hairs that trap particles and 'flick' them away just as you would a bit of dust from your shirt or blouse. This is the basis of a sneeze, in which the whole system works in unison to get rid of irritants.

The Specialist Protectors – Bioflavonoids and Beta-Carotene

In 1524 a French explorer, Jacques Cartier, and his men had to spend the winter on board ship in the Canadian St Lawrence Seaway with only salt pork to eat. The men started to come down with scurvy, a vitamin C deficiency disease which was in those days fatal. Friendly Indians showed Cartier how to brew a tea from pine needles that alleviated and prevented scurvy. It saved Cartier and his men from disaster. The explorers survived the winter in good health and sailed back to France in the spring.

Until around 1985, scientists thought the tea prevented scurvy because it contained vitamin C. Then a Dr Jacques Mescalier re-examined Cartier's experience. He knew that the boiling water used to make tea destroys vitamin C, and that pine needles don't contain any vitamin C in the first place.

Mescalier proved that a bioflavonoid, specifically called pycnogenol, in the needles was responsible for curing scurvy. This bioflavonoid is thirty to fifty times more effective as an antioxidant than vitamin C. About one gram of pycnogenol provides the same protection as fifty grams of vitamin C. Therefore, because the bioflavonoids react more readily with free radicals than vitamin C, they protect vitamin C from oxidation and save even the most minute amount. Only ten milligrams of vitamin C prevents scurvy under most conditions, but if you add the bioflavonoids, possibly five milligrams or less of vitamin C is required. It took almost 500 years to recognise that bioflavonoids are such important antioxidants. We also realise why people who drink a modest amount of red wine regularly may be protecting themselves against heart disease. When it begins, heart disease is partly an unwanted oxidative process, and the bioflavonoids that start in the grapes are passed into the wine where they act as a protector antioxidant.

Bioflavonoids are found in all fruits and vegetables. Citrus fruits are particularly rich in them, especially in the white membranes of oranges, tangerines and grapefruit. The name comes from 'bio', meaning biological in origin, and 'flavonoid' which refers to a member of a group of aromatic compounds. These compounds have a common chemical structure, called a flavine, which is an especially good antioxidant. The flavine structure is widely used in nature.

Until around 1990, scientists knew that bioflavonoids existed in foods, but their antioxidant role was not fully appreciated. Now our knowledge of free radicals and unwanted oxidative processes has reached a level where the value of all antioxidants, including bioflavonoids, is recognised. Bioflavonoids are seen as part of nature's antioxidant defence-strategy and are recognised as being a prime source of protection. In fact there are so many of them that it will be years before they are all understood.

Building your Antioxidant Reservoir

The antioxidant level of your body is determined by the foods you eat. But the things you do, the place you live and to some extent the family you come from can all influence your need for antioxidants. The size of your antioxidant reservoir and the eating habits that replenish it helps explain why some smokers have more wrinkled skin than others and why some smokers get cataracts and other problems when others stay immune.

The findings about antioxidants allow us to pinpoint exact dietary changes. Basically I feel we have to emphasise eating the correct food over and above taking supplements, although the two should work together. Since so many antioxidants are not yet identified, we would do better to choose the foods we know are rich in protective qualities rather than relying on supplements which may only provide us with part of the picture.

Smokers have special needs. Studies of vitamin C, the simplest of all antioxidants, indicate that people who smoke have much lower blood levels of vitamin C than non-smokers. This finding supports two conclusions. First we know smoke contains oxidising agents that are neutralised by vitamin C, causing the vitamin C to be destroyed in the process. Second, we know from many surveys that smokers don't eat the correct amounts of fruit and vegetables, which means their blood levels of vitamin C will be low from diet alone.

Estimates show that smokers need about 330 per cent more vitamin C than non-smokers. This is consistent with its front-line role as an antioxidant. However, keep in mind that what can be said for vitamin C holds true for all other antioxidants, such as beta carotene. Vitamin C gets our attention because it's a nutrient that is easily studied and widely known.

Here's how to start your antioxidant routine NOW:

- Eat deep green, dark red, orange or yellow vegetables: three to five servings daily
- Eat fruits with red, yellow, orange or green flesh: three to five servings daily
- If you are a coffee drinker, choose tea in place of coffee for one cup daily. Evidence indicates tea is better than coffee.
- Drink coloured fruit juices: natural juice, such as orange, cranberry, melon, papaya and the like.
- Take supplements of one gram vitamin C a day. Make sure the supplement contains bioflavonoids.
- Take up to 25 mg of beta carotene daily in addition to lots of coloured vegetables.
- Take between 100 and 1,500 IU of Vitamin E per day.

CHAPTER THREE

Vital Protection with Antioxidants

How easy it would be if we could put all the antioxidants we need in a single daily capsule or drink. Unfortunately that's not possible, because our antioxidant needs are extensive and ever-changing, and there are so many antioxidants to deal with.

Science has discovered many characteristics about antioxidants. For example, while vitamin C is a single material, vitamin E consists of about eight variants. Because vitamins C and E are protected by bioflavonoids, it's important to get them together. Selecting the correct foods and food supplements calls for planning. This chapter will identify the major antioxidants, antioxidant foods and a strategy that can be used for meal, snack and supplement selection.

Vitamin C and Bioflavonoids

Vitamin C is the simplest of all the nutrient antioxidants. Chemically, it's a single material named ascorbic acid, which comes from the word 'ascorbutin' because it cured the disease scurvy. Scurvy is the result of a longstanding vitamin C deficiency. Today we know vitamin C is both an important general nutrient and an antioxidant that prevents many illnesses and can slow the aging process. As an antioxidant, vitamin C helps prevent cancer, heart disease, skin wrinkles and other cosmetic and health problems.

Bioflavonoids are found in most vitamin C-rich foods, such as fruits and vegetables. They enhance the action of vitamin C and serve as antioxidants in their own right.

Smokers can maintain the same vitamin C blood levels as nonsmokers if they get at least 200 mg daily. But there's more. Recent research shows that non-smokers need even more vitamin C as an antioxidant. The normal recommendations focus on vitamin C's role in metabolism – not as an antioxidant. We need at least 300 mg daily as a general requirement, and smokers need between 500 mg and 1,000 mg (one gram) daily.

Heavy smokers, however, have an even larger vitamin C requirement. And as we age, our bodies also need more vitamin C to keep its reservoirs at the same level. So a 60-year-old moderately heavy smoker would need around 1,500 mg of vitamin C daily. It's actually cheaper and more practical to get that much vitamin C from supplements than to try to get it from food.

Table 3.1 lists the best food sources of vitamin C. I have omitted acerola (a kind of cherry) from the list even though its fruit provides 1,644 mg per serving and its juice 3,800 mg per serving. However, the acerola is not a common food and the likelihood of your consuming it every day is slight!

TABLE 3.1 *Fruit, vegetable and juice sources of vitamin C in milligrams (mg)*

Fruits

25–45 mg	50–95 mg	100–200 mg
Breadfruit	Cantaloupe	Blackcurrants
Carambola	Elderberries	Guava
Currants	Jujube	Papaya
(red and white)	Kiwi fruit	Pomelo
Gooseberries	Lychees	
Grapefruit	Mango	
Honeydew melon	Mulberries	
Lemon	Orange, navel	
Mandarin orange	Orange, valencia	
Tangerine	Strawberries	

Vegetables

25–45 mg	50–100 mg
Broccoli	Pepper (hot)
Brussels sprouts	Pepper,
Cassava	sweet green
Cauliflower	Pepper,
Dock	sweet red
Kale	
Onions	
Parsley	
Peas	
Seaweed (Nori)	
Sweet potato	

Fresh or Frozen Juices

25–45 mg	50–95 mg	100–200 mg
Pineapple	Grape	Cranberry
Tomato	Lime	Grapefruit
	Passionfruit	Lemon
	Tangerine	Orange
	V-8 juice	

Note: Quantities of foods listed to provide the amount of vitamin C shown are four ounces (100 g). All juice servings are half a pint (0.3 litres).

Fruit, vegetables and juices will obviously go some way towards fulfilling your vitamin C requirement. But I would strongly urge you also to take an additional supplement of 500 to 1,000 mg of vitamin C daily, making sure that the one you choose is sugar-free and contains bioflavonoids.

Carotenoids and Beta Carotene

Carotenoids are pigments found in all plants. Over 865 carotenoids are known and the list keeps growing. All carotenoids are antioxidants, but beta carotene is the most common carotenoid and is essential to green plants and to humans. It is found in all green plants such as spinach, and orange and yellow plants, such as carrots and melons.

Beta carotene and some of the other carotenoids are converted to vitamin A as our body's needs call for it.

About six milligrams of beta carotene daily are usually enough. Anything more remains as beta carotene without being converted to vitamin A and increases our antioxidant reservoir. Most people's diets supply just about enough beta carotene daily, which gives us enough vitamin A but doesn't leave any left over for beta carotenes's natural antioxidant protection. Evidence is increasingly showing that 25 mg of beta carotene daily is a good protective level. Beta carotene is completely safe (unlike straight vitamin A, which can be toxic in large doses), even though an excess of it may give your skin an orange tinge.

All the studies conducted on tobacco-users have confirmed the protective role of beta carotene. A paper published in the journal *Nature* in 1980 by Dr Bob Shekelle showed that heavy smokers who ate sufficient beta carotene-rich foods, such as dark green and orange vegetables, had dramatically reduced rates of lung cancer. Shekelle's work started extensive research on beta carotene. American trials on tobacco chewers in the 1980s showed that 25 mg of beta carotene daily reduced the formation of precancerous mouth lesions by over 50 per cent. Some precancerous cells became normal again.

Dr K Fred Gey at the University of Berne, in Switzerland, concluded from all the available information that a non-smoker needs 15 mg of beta carotene daily to achieve an optimum beta carotene reservoir. But common sense dictates that a heavy smoker needs a higher intake – and direct studies on stomach and lung cancer in smokers helped Dr Gey to reach this conclusion. A large study focusing on heart attack and stroke in the United States used 25 mg of beta carotene a day with outstanding results.

From these studies I conclude that a smoker, passive smoker and people who work and commute in urban areas should strive for 20 mg of beta carotene daily, while 25 mg a day would provide even better protection. As far as beta carotene is concerned, it's a case of 'more is better'.

Beta carotene is outstandingly useful amongst the carotenoids, but others are also important. Carotenoids generally seem to protect in particular the organs with exposed surfaces, such as the skin, lungs, eyes and mouth.

Lycopene, a red carotenoid, has been found to reduce the risk of bladder cancer. Smokers have an above-normal risk of bladder cancer. Eating foods specifically rich in lycopene, such as a salad of tomatoes and red peppers, reduces your risk of this disease to near-average. Lycopene illustrates an important point: you can't rely on beta carotene supplements alone – the full range of carotenoids is necessary. Thus you have to get a diet of foods rich in carotenoids as well as using supplements.

To consume the correct amount of carotenoids, then, I recommend:

- Eat four servings of deep green, yellow or red vegetables every day, selected from table 3.2. A mixture of all of them is preferable.
- Eat the equivalent of 4 oz (100 g) of tomatoes daily as sauce or cut up in a salad.

- Eat three servings daily of coloured fruit such as melon, oranges, strawberries, plums, per day.

TABLE 3.2 *Foods rich in carotenoids (4oz/100g serving)*

Less than 2 mg	2–5 mg	Over 5 mg
Vegetables		
Avocado	Beetroot greens	Carrots
Broccoli	Chicory	Sweetcorn
Cabbage	Collards	Pumpkin
Chard, Swiss	Dandelion greens	Spinach
Mustard greens	Dock	Sweet potato
Spring onions	Kale	
Tomato (red)	Mustard spinach	
	Peppers (sweet red)	
	Seaweed (Nori)	
	Marrows	
	Tomato paste	
	Turnip greens	
Fruits		
Apricots	Cantaloupe	
Cherries	Mango	
Mandarin orange	Papaya	
Nectarine	Persimmon	
Peaches		
Prunes (10)		

Vitamin E

Vitamin E is actually the collective capacity of eight materials, four tocopherols and four tocotrienols, known as alpha, beta, gamma and delta. Not all of them metabolise in the body as vitamin E, but all of them are antioxidants.

We don't know everything there is to know about the protective effects of the tocopherols and tocotrienols. But we do know that they work as antioxidants in many ways in many parts of the body. For example, one tocopherol might work best in the alveolar tissue of the lung but not be able to enter some other tissue. A vitamin E supplement should therefore contain a mixture of tocopherols and tocotrienols.

Vitamin E protects oils from oxidation. Like all antioxidants, vitamin E is sacrificed to save other, more important materials. Vitamin E is never very plentiful in the diet, but smokers can't possibly get enough from their food. Because the vitamin E requirement increases with smoking and urban life, we must rely on supplements.

Research indicates that normal vitamin E requirement is at least 50 IU daily. Indeed, K Fred Gey and his colleagues at Berne in Switzerland concluded that between 60 and 100 IU of vitamin E is necessary to build and maintain an adequate vitamin E antioxidant reservoir. Only two foods could supply that much vitamin E: wheat germ oil or wheat germ itself. Most people don't eat enough wheat germ regularly to reach that level. So supplements are the only answer.

Children of smokers aren't likely to get enough vitamin E to protect them either. They should also take supplements.

We know that vitamin E can protect against lung cancer and emphysema – problems related to smoking and air pollution. Seen another way, people with low vitamin E levels are at greater risk of getting these diseases. Studies of cataracts have given us even better information. In one study, 400 IU of vitamin E daily reduced cataract formation by 60 per cent. Research supporting these findings comes from many countries. The eyes benefit in other ways from vitamin E – it protects the delicate oils in the retina from damage. It is also the only known antioxidant to prevent nerve damage and stop age spots forming.

Biochemists explain the relationship between disease and vitamin E as follows. Vitamin E protects delicate oils that are essential parts of cell membranes and other tissue protectors, such as omega-3 oils, which are essential to nerve tissues and healthy metabolism. When these oils, tissues and membranes are attacked by free radicals, the cells and tissues are damaged and made vulnerable to attack by other toxins. Vitamin E is an essential component of the fluids that bathe delicate tissues, especially the alveolar fluid of the lungs. So vitamin E protects these tissues from the irritation caused by smoking. This protection extends against asthma, to which children and people who live in cities are vulnerable. Not surprisingly, the children of smokers are more likely to develop asthma and emphysema.

How much vitamin E should you aim to take, then? Strive for at least 100 IU daily. Indeed, it's better for smokers and passive smokers – including children – to take 400 IU. Wheat germ and wheat germ oil are the richest and most practical sources. Adding wheat germ to foods such as cereals and salads is an excellent health practice. Similarly, vitamin E supplements should include wheat germ oil. Vitamin E is non-toxic and human use up to 4,000 IU daily has been proven safe in clinical research.

Selenium

In contrast to the tocopherols and tocotrienols, selenium is a trace mineral, meaning that we need very little of it. Selenium and vitamin E work together, which is unexpected because chemically they are completely different. However, it has been found that selenium and vitamin E have an equal ability to destroy free radicals, and they each work in different places in a living cell.

Vitamin E and selenium are front-line antioxidants on the surface of each cell. As you move away from the site of each nutrient on the cell surface, its protective effects weaken. However, the region where the weak area of one overlaps with the weak area of the other is more strongly protected. This overlapping area increases the protection of each nutrient beyond the boundaries you'd expect from each nutrient alone. Hence the combined action of vitamin E and selenium is greater than either one's individual effect.

We need very little selenium, and an excessive amount can be toxic. The RNI for selenium is 75 micrograms daily for men, and 60 for women. Smokers should strive for 50 to 100 per cent more than the RNI. If you take 70 micrograms as a supplement, your diet will provide the excess. Seventy micrograms is so small that it is almost invisible. Now you see what we mean by the word 'trace'.

The best way to get enough selenium is to make sure your daily multi-vitamin and multi-mineral supplement contains 100 per cent of the RNI. In addition to that, eat some of the selenium-rich foods listed in Table 3:3. Don't rush out and buy selenium supplements thinking that if a little is good, more must be better. That can lead to serious trouble.

TABLE 3.3 *Food sources of selenium*

Good Sources 5–15 mcg	*Better Sources* 20–45 mcg	*Best Sources* 50–100 mcg
Cereals, 3.5 oz.	Fish, 3.5 oz.	Egg noodles, 3.5 oz.
Dairy products, 8 oz.	Meat, 3.5 oz.	
	Poultry, 3.5 oz.	Pasta, 3.5 oz.
Eggs, 1 medium	Rice, ½ cup	Shellfish, 3.5 oz.
Vegetables, 3.5 oz.	Wholewheat bread, 1 slice	
White bread, 1 slice		

Note: Values cited are averages. 3.5 oz. = just under 100 g

Brassicas – Nature's Special Protectors

Eat your broccoli! Finish that cabbage! Those Brussels sprouts are good for you! Sounds familiar? Throughout the ages mothers have urged their children to eat these vegetables from the brassica family – and children have continually resisted them. That's how characters such as 'Popeye' began. They were usually 'heroes' invented to get children interested in vegetables.

Mother's advice was sound. Brassicas are the oldest of all cultivated vegetables, and since the early Roman era their health properties have been renowned. The link between these vegetables and smoking first appeared when scientists found that the risk of lung cancer in heavy smokers declined when they ate Brussels sprouts. Since the late 1970s numerous studies on all types of cancer in smokers have verified the protective effect of brassicas and similar vegetables.

Smokers who eat more brassicas have less incidence of cancer, fewer serious digestive problems and better health in general. These benefits are derived from the unique antioxidants in the brassicas that in turn induce the body to heighten its own defences. So as protective foods, brassicas work in two ways: they provide antioxidants and they cause your body to build a stronger defence network.

Neutralising some free radical producers called superoxides calls for an enzyme named superoxide dismutase, or SOD. Brassicas induce the body to make more SOD. SOD uses substances from brassicas, such as indoles and phenols among many others to neutralise free radicals. Think of SOD as a bomb disposal expert, using materials from brassicas to neutralise the bomb.

If you like brassicas, this is all good news. But if you prefer to get your nutrition from supplements, you've got a problem. Supplements of the materials from these sort of vegetables aren't available and probably never will be available. So this is one case where more is definitely better, and there's no such thing as 'too much'.

TABLE 3.4 *Brassicas*

Broccoli	Japanese horseradish
Brussels sprouts	Kale
Cabbage (red, white, and others)	Kohlrabi
	Mustard
Cauliflower	Radish
Chinese cabbage (bok choy)	Swede
Cress	Turnip
Horseradish	Watercress

As an incentive to eat more brassicas, Table 3:5 lists the cancers they can help prevent. As all these cancers are initiated by free radicals, it follows that the brassicas will help prevent other problems initiated by free radical damage and accelerated by smoking such as cataracts, emphysema, asthma, age spots and wrinkles.

TABLE 3.5 *Cancer risks reduced by increased intake of brassicas*

Aerodigestive
Breast
Colorectal
Lung
Pancreatic
Prostate
Stomach

Garlic and Onions

In 1550BC an Egyptian papyrus, the Codex Ebers, laid out the therapeutic and preventive properties of garlic. Garlic was widely used in the ancient world as an antibacterial and antifungal agent, a vermifuge (against intestinal worms), a tumour preventive and a cure for 'hot blood'. During World War I, garlic was one of the most effective materials available for sterilising open wounds. By the 1940s antibiotics derived from moulds were discovered and became more economical, so garlic fell into disuse. Ancient practices died quickly and became the material of folklore.

While searching for antibiotics in 1944, Dr Chester Cavalito, a scientist working in Buffalo in the United States, proved that garlic had real anti-bacterial and anti-viral properties. In fact, garlic is better than penicillin at killing some bacteria. For some fungal infections and viruses, garlic is still the preferred treatment. Garlic's anti-tumour properties have been proven effective and are currently being researched worldwide.

We know that garlic is an excellent source of unique antioxidants, and the same can be said for onions, leeks, shallots and other edible bulbs. In addition, materials in garlic help modulate high blood pressure – which we can assume was the 'hot blood' referred to by the ancients.

Onions, which belong to the same family, have many of garlic's properties, as well as one that garlic seems to lack: the ability to prevent high blood sugar levels. While the active substance that has this effect hasn't been identified, the ability has been clinically verified. In addition, the anti-bacterial properties of these unique vegetables help us fight infection and colds.

Putting Antioxidants Together

Making antioxidants work for you requires a combination of good food selection and effective supplement use. Let the following lists of foods and food supplements guide your choice.

Food

- Fruits: At least three servings daily with one vitamin C-rich fruit eaten raw.
- Vegetables: At least three servings a day, with one including a red or orange vegetable. Your selection should also include brassicas, the more the better.

- Grains and cereals: one serving of a cereal containing wheat germ, or with wheat germ added to it.
- Garlic, onions and edible bulbs: each day you should eat one of these in a salad, sauce or cooked dish.

Supplements

- Vitamin C: at least 500 mg daily in a supplement that contains at least 100 mg of bioflavonoids
- Beta carotene: At least 25 mg daily in a supplement
- Vitamin E: at least 100 IU or more in a supplement that contains a mixture of tocopherols and tocotrienols, preferably in wheat germ oil.

Cancer-Fighting
with the B-Team

Do you think that people either have cancer or they don't? If you answered 'Yes' – you're wrong. This chapter helps you understand how cancer starts and gives an insight into how you can reduce the risk factors. What's valid for cancer protection is also effective for preventing emphysema and other benign but equally degenerative side effects of smoking.

The 50 trillion body cells reproduce, on average, about every seven weeks. So, in a sense, we're always about seven weeks old, except for our brain cells and some others which don't reproduce. But don't panic! We've got enough extra brain cells to live over 150 years. When something goes wrong with a cell's genetic material, it can become a cancer cell. Once the cell becomes cancerous and continues to reproduce, cancer has started. If the immune system's special 'killer' cells don't recognise and kill the cancer cells, cancer has started growing.

However, there is an intermediate stage when a cell is not normal, but it's not a cancer cell either. At this stage, medical scientists call it a precancerous cell, or, more scientifically, a dysplastic cell. Think of a ruler that's labelled 'normal' at one end and 'cancer' at the other. The area in between the two is the dysplastic phase.

A cell can survive in this dysplastic phase for a long time. A good example is intestinal polyps, which are clumps of dysplastic cells on the inside lining of the large intestine. The longer the polyps are there, the more likely it is that the cells in them will become cancerous. Scientists have learned that two per cent of polyps become cancerous in five years, and 24 per cent in 20 years, with various levels of development in between. Similar statistics apply to polyps in other places, such as nasal passages and on vocal cords. Cancer is only certain when a clear diagnosis has been made. Up till that point, doctors can only speak of risk. So, the objective is to minimise the risk.

A number of factors accelerate the rate at which a cell moves through the dysplastic phase to become cancerous. In the intestines, some major factors include a lack of dietary fibre, too much dietary fat, tobacco use, alcohol use, and lack of folic acid (a B vitamin).

The Foliage Factor: Folic Acid

Folic acid is one of seven B vitamins. Its name comes from its source – green leafy vegetables, such as spinach. Once it was scientifically identified, the name folacin was used. Because folacin in its free form is an acid, it's also called folic acid.

Folic acid deficiency is characterised by the famous 'Popeye' cartoons. If you remember, Popeye would get weak, tired and mentally confused. When he was in this state, his arch-rival Bluto could get the better of him, usually by stealing his girlfriend, Olive Oyl. But as soon as Popeye ate his spinach, his strength returned and he would 'mop the floor' with Bluto.

We no longer see serious folic acid deficiencies like Popeye's sad state, despite the fact that our diet rarely supplies enough of this nutrient. Smokers' diets are especially lacking in it. Recently, though, scientists discovered something very important. Even though a shortfall – i.e. less than the RNI – may not be large enough to create deficiency symptoms, a cell without enough folic acid is more likely to become dysplastic. That's not surprising, because folic acid is required for correct cellular reproduction, and works at the most basic level of all: where genetic material is manufactured.

The first eight weeks of pregnancy is a time when the foetus is particularly sensitive to folic acid deficiencies. This is a time of very rapid growth, especially of the face, spine and brain. Women who are short of folic acid during this time are more likely to give birth to a child with a cleft palate, spinal deformity, or even more serious brain damage. But these women do not lack enough folic acid to be classed as having a deficiency. Recent findings suggest that these women don't convert the storage form, folacin, to the active form, folic acid, fast enough to meet the demands of early pregnancy.

Armed with this knowledge about birth defects, scientists reasoned that a shortage of folic acid could cause dysplastic cells in adults. They have confirmed that folic acid shortfall accelerates the transition of cells in intestinal and other polyps to cancer cells. This finding is especially important for smokers. Oxidising agents, found in tobacco smoke, deplete folic acid. To make matters worse, smokers' diets are usually short on vegetables, and smokers don't eat enough folic acid-rich foods to make up for the depletion.

Smokers usually have some dysplastic cells on the lining of their bronchial tubes. They can be clumped into polyps on those tissues, similar to polyps on the intestines. In one study, scientists gave smokers folic acid supplements. Fewer dysplastic cells were observed in their bronchial tubes and other aerodigestive tissues (tissues that are exposed to air and food). The longer the smokers took folic acid, the fewer dysplastic cells they had. The conclusion was clear: folic acid helps reverse dysplasia in delicate bronchial tissues, especially when it is caused by smoking, airborne environmental pollutants and other forms of irritants.

In another study, scientists showed that where there was a lack of folic acid in the intestinal tissues, a higher rate of colorectal cancer occurred. If the people who were likely to have depleted folic acid used folic acid supplements, their colorectal cancer rate dropped by about 15 per cent.

Now, remember that smokers don't usually take in the RNI for folic acid and therefore are deficient in this important vitamin all the time. Even though they may be just a little bit short, the deficiency can cause serious trouble.

Smokers and those who associate with them, then, should eat plenty of spinach, broccoli and other good sources of folic acid. You can also take a folic acid supplement with the other B vitamins. However, I haven't finished telling you about the B vitamins yet, because you also need other members of the team. Supplements should always be balanced with all the B vitamins.

Niacin

Until recently niacin was considered a relatively unimportant member of the B vitamin family. Like all the B vitamins, it was thought to be helpful for general health and metabolic efficiency. More niacin is called for when you're especially active, which is how it was discovered as lacking in the diets of female athletes.

Now scientists have acknowledged that niacin has a very special role. It is an essential member of a system that repairs mistakes in our genetic material. This system, DNA polymerase, corrects mistakes in the substance on which cell reproduction depends. No clear relationship between niacin and cancer has been established yet, but the research is still going on. Some interesting protective relationships have been discovered, however. Dairy products and meat have shown a minor protective effect against cancer. Both are good sources of niacin. Since smokers are at greater risk of having dysplastic cells, so it makes sense that they get a higher intake of folic acid and niacin.

As with many nutrients, you may find interchangeable names for niacin. It can be referred to as niacinamide, nicotinamide or nicotinic acid (no relation to nicotine!)

The Complete B-Family

All B vitamins have essential roles in nutrition and health. Most of them are vitally involved in metabolic processes and the conversion of food chemicals into energy. Therefore all the B vitamins are important for good health, energy, mental outlook and tissue repair. A couple of the B vitamins – biotin and pantothenic acid – are also critical for the work of some antioxidants, giving them a specialised protective role.

Let's look at what the B complex vitamins do, and then I'll explain why they're especially important to smokers. All the B vitamins share common characteristics:

- They are essential for the release of energy from food.
- They are essential for the complex chemical processes that take place in the body's cells.
- They are essential for the maintenance of physical and mental fitness, healthy skin, hair, eyes, nerves and all the body tissues.
- The absence of any one for long enough can cause death.
- Most B vitamins are destroyed by processing, which includes heat, storage and even light.

Table 4:1 lists the B complex of vitamins and the amounts required daily.

TABLE 4.1 *B-complex vitamins*

Vitamin	RDA
B$_6$*	2.2 milligrams
B$_{12}$	3.0 micrograms
Biotin*	65 micrograms
Folic acid or folacin	400 micrograms
Niacin	19 milligrams
Pantothenic acid*	6.5 milligrams
Riboflavin (B$_2$)	1.7 milligrams
Thiamine (B$_1$)	1.5 milligrams

*No RDA is established.

Smoking and Weight – A Metabolic Problem

Smokers have a higher basal metabolic rate than non-smokers, meaning that all their body processes tend to work more quickly. Since the B complex vitamins are directly involved in the metabolism, it follows that smokers need more of them for this reason too.

Indirect proof of this increased metabolic rate comes from the fact that smokers on average weigh less than people who don't smoke. It seems that smokers burn more of their food calories. I speculate that another reason for lower weight is that smokers' metabolisms are less efficient because their diets are more poorly balanced. Dietary balance is hard to study. Poor dietary balance includes the fact that some of the B vitamins may be out of proportion. Because these nutrients influence the metabolic rate, any imbalance upsets the metabolic efficiency.

Evidence that smokers need more of the B vitamins comes from a study of people who stopped smoking and carefully maintained exactly the same eating habits they had as smokers. These ex-smokers put on weight, even though they didn't increase their food intake. This carefully researched finding is proof that the metabolic rate slows to normal after people stop smoking, and that the metabolic rate was higher when they smoked. The slower metabolic rate means that the body is burning fewer calories in order to keep working, and the extra calories are available for storage as fat. Bodies don't waste surplus energy – they store it as fat for hard times.

Substituting one form of oral gratification – food – for another is often a reason smokers give for putting on weight when they stop. But clearly this is not necessarily the case.

Mental Outlook

Smokers often defend themselves by saying that they concentrate better and feel more mentally alert after a cigarette. This could suggest that people who smoke are suffering from mild depression, since their mental capacities decline without the mood-elevating cigarettes.

Although no serious clinical studies on mental health have proved that depressed people improve when they take more vitamin B, there is indirect evidence that this is so. If you accept that smokers have a tendency to mild depression, and also recognise that any shortage of the B vitamins shows up as depression, confusion and general slowness, then you can see why there is such a good case for extra B complex vitamins for smokers.

B-Complex Supplements

I favour a general supplement that supplies 100 per cent of the RNI of the B complex vitamins for average people. For smokers and those around them, I recommend extra B complex. In selecting a good B complex supplement, make sure that:

- All the B vitamins are in the amounts shown in the RNI chart (table 4.1 above).
- The supplement contains biotin and pantothenic acid within 50 per cent of the levels shown in table 4.1 even though there is no RNI for these nutrients.

CHAPTER FIVE

Deep Cleansing with Dietary Fibre

If your diet includes enough fruit, vegetables and cereals you should get about 30 grams of fibre daily, the dietary reference value (DRV) recommended for average adults. If you smoke, you should strive for at least this and preferably more per day.

The average daily consumption of fibre in the UK is around 12 grams. In other words, we get only two-thirds of what we need. Because we know that smokers tend to eat fewer vegetables than other people, we can infer that they get much less than this already below-requirements amount. The consequences are serious.

Constipation is the clearest outcome of inadequate dietary fibre. Constipation can be defined as infrequent bowel movements – in other words, less than every 24 to 36 hours. Most authorities say that optimum bowel function is a light-brown movement once every 24 hours, which requires about 30 grams of fibre daily. Constipation contributes to poor complexion, abdominal discomfort, digestive disorders and several types of cancer. It has been linked directly to many intestinal disorders, including ulcers, gallstones, diverticulosis, irritable bowel syndrome, colitis, haemorrhoids, varicose veins and colorectal cancer. Smoking exaggerates the risk of each of these illnesses.

What is Dietary Fibre?

Fibre is the indigestible material from plant foods, including cereals, grains, vegetables and fruit. The British Nutrition Foundation has recommended that the term 'fibre' should become obsolete, preferring to use 'NSP' (non-starch polysaccharides), but it is likely to remain in general use for some time yet.

Different foods provide different types of fibre, classified as either soft or hard. Soft fibre is also called soluble fibre, and hard fibre is called insoluble fibre. Hard fibre increases the bulk of bowel material and soft fibre increases its water content, also helping bind and remove toxic wastes. You need about three times as much insoluble fibre as soluble. 'Soluble' simply means that the food material dissolves in water – for example, sugar – while insoluble materials remain in their fibrous state.

All plant foods provide both soluble and insoluble fibre, but some plants are richer in one type than another. For example, wheat bran is almost completely insoluble fibre, while apple pectin is almost all soluble fibre. That's why people should eat a wide variety of plant foods to try to consume the recommended daily requirement.

Table 5.1 lists the effects of fibre on stool volume and also the ability of these fibres to lower cholesterol. Hard fibre, such as from wheat bran, increases stool volume most, but all fibres do this to some extent. By increasing stool volume you improve bowel regularity and move more water through your digestive system. Together these effects improve your health by helping rid your body of waste products quickly. Lowering cholesterol is another means of helping to detoxify the body.

TABLE 5.1 *Fibre input: stool output*

Fibre Source	Fibre Type	Stool Volume Increase per Unit of Fibre	Cholesterol-lowering Ability
Wheat Bran, raw or cooked	Hard	5.7	None
Fruits and vegetables: carrots, cabbage, peas, apple, beans, etc.	Mixed	4.9	Fair
Oats: oat bran; rolled oats	More soft	3.9	Excellent
Gums and mucilages: psyllium, guar, sterculia	Soft	3.5	Excellent
Corn: corn bran, cornmeal	More soft	3.4	Good

Getting Adequate Fibre

We can be short of most nutrients without ever knowing it. Even the results of serious vitamin deficiencies don't usually appear for several months. Vitamin shortages can usually be corrected easily. But fibre is more difficult. When it is deficient, we become accustomed to not getting enough and not having regular bowel movements. Or we take laxatives and think they solve matters, when all they do is cover up the problem. Chronic fibre deficiencies show up in 20 or more years as serious bowel disorders such as diverticulosis or even cancer. They can also contribute to indirect effects of toxic overloading such as asthma or arthritis. You will know you are getting adequate amounts of fibre when your bowel movements become regular and easy.

Fibre and Polyps

In Chapter 4 I mentioned that intestinal polyps are clumps of dysplastic cells with a high probability of becoming cancerous if you have them long enough. A diet with adequate fibre prevents polyp formation. Some research indicates that fibre actually helps make polyps disappear after they have formed. They come and go with adequate fibre, but they come and stay with inadequate fibre.

Now, add to this knowledge the fact that smokers have a higher risk of intestinal or colorectal cancer. This means that tars and other materials from cigarettes which get into the system probably accelerate the transition of polyps to a cancerous state. In my opinion, this should be a sufficient reason for smokers to switch to a high-fibre diet.

Fibre - Nature's Detoxifier

Dietary fibre, especially soluble fibre, combines with unwanted material and helps the body detoxify itself. Many of these 'toxins' are by-products of liver metabolism or materials trapped by the liver. They pass into the intestinal tract through the bile duct. This duct connects the gall bladder, which is the liver's toxic waste dump, to the intestines. If these wastes aren't taken up by dietary fibre, many of them become reabsorbed further along in the digestive system. Then they can move via the blood and lymphatic systems to all parts of the body.

If the body is working correctly, it will also convert cholesterol to waste material – bile acid – through the bile duct and remove it from the system. Then there is less chance of cholesterol building up to create 'sludge' in the arteries. Good cholesterol-lowering strategies include higher-fibre (especially soluble fibre) low-fat diets. Oatmeal, beans and some vegetable gums are particularly good at lowering cholesterol. You may also want to include some fibre in supplement form, usually sold as psyllium or linseeds in health food stores.

Clinical studies have verified the ability of fibre to remove toxins from the body. Constipated people cannot eliminate toxins properly. Consequently, they have a higher risk of many illnesses, such as asthma, heart disease, high blood pressure, cancer and intestinal disorders. Frequency and volume of bowel movements go together to produce the most efficient body waste removal system. Prevention is the best cure and merely calls for enough dietary fibre.

Fibre and Smokers

Smoking increases the risk of many stomach and bowel disorders, but none are so ominous as pancreatic, stomach and colo-rectal cancer. The risk of any of these can be reduced with enough fibre. Following a good food and fibre-supplement programme will improve your health and remove several major risks from your life.

Fibre in Cereals

Any supermarket offers an array of cereals that make starting each day with high fibre intake very easy. A good fibre cereal will provide a considerable part of your requirements for the day – 7–12 grams or more per serving. A word of warning: many proprietary brands of cereal have a high sugar content. Choose low-sugar or sugar-free varieties if possible. There are also many excellent recipes for making your own muesli or granola cereals from mixtures of grains and dried fruits found in health food stores.

Fibre in Fruit

Fruit is also a good source of fibre and if you eat enough of it you will be well on your way to a high-fibre diet. Snack on an apple or pear, for example, and you'll get around 1.6 grams of fibre.

Fibre in Vegetables

Smokers should increase their vegetable intake, as I keep emphasising. As well as providing a wealth of antioxidants, vegetables will add to your daily complement of dietary fibre.

Vegetables usually contain more soluble than insoluble fibre. You can easily supply 30 to 50 per cent of your daily fibre needs through vegetables. Try snacking on carrots in between meals to set yourself off to a good start!

Fibre Supplements

Despite your best efforts, you still might not eat enough fibre to guarantee your daily needs. Therefore you can use fibre supplements to increase that amount. Your health food shop should be able to provide these. It is absolutely essential to use fibre supplements with plenty of water. Fibre without water can create serious constipation. That's why it is best to obtain your fibre the natural way, from a balanced diet.

You can supplement with fibre by purchasing a supplement designed specifically for the purpose. Fibre supplements are usually made from psyllium husks. Unprocessed wheat bran can be used in recipes, but is not a good supplement.

Bread

Most bread supplies very little fibre. Always buy bread made from whole grain if possible – not just 'brown' bread. Proper whole grain bread should contain at least a gram of fibre in two slices.

High Fibre Diets

A 'high fibre' diet is really a misnomer. None of us is likely to consume a truly high amount of fibre. As nations industrialise, the fibre content of their diet declines. In Europe of 1850, the average diet provided over 12 grams of fibre per 1,000 calories. In those days, women consumed over 2,000 calories a day and men over 3,000. So on average their diets provided a really high fibre diet. In our society, where we get under the amount of fibre our bodies need, what we call a 'high fibre' diet is just an adequate-fibre diet. Invest in eating foods that supply enough fibre – the return is well worth it. And remember, foods that contain fibre will also contribute to your vitamin, mineral and antioxidant needs.

- Start every day with a good high-fibre cereal.
- Eat fruit and cut-up raw vegetables as between-meal snacks.

- Eat plentiful helpings of vegetables at least twice a day.
- Use fibre supplements if you suspect your fibre intake is not sufficient.

CHAPTER SIX

Stroke and Heart Attack – Foiled by Fish Fat

Watch how a simple cut or scratch heals, and you will have an insight into the process leading to a heart attack. Specialised blood cells clump together to block the break in the small blood vessels at the site of the wound. If you look at it through a microscope, a tiny scratch is like a large hole, so it takes a good-sized clump to seal it. The clot which then forms is a marvellous, complex process and also one of nature's best-organised defensive processes at work. Strokes and most heart attacks result from the same process. But in these cases, the clot forms in the wrong place at the wrong time.

A stroke or a myocardial infarction – that's a heart attack caused by a clot or another sort of lump blocking a blood vessel in the heart – begins in precisely the same way as the clot which closes a scratch. Blood cells clump together because of some disturbance and the whole process begins. If a clot blocks a vessel in the brain, then it can lead to a stroke. If it blocks a vessel in the heart, it means a heart attack. An internal clot can happen at any age but is unusual before the age of 60. Among the many factors that increase the risk of an internal clot, smoking tops the list.

It does so because gases in smoke – mostly carbon monoxide – make the blood more sticky and able to clump together more easily. Scientifically speaking, carbon monoxide increases blood platelet adhesiveness and aggregation.

Reducing High Blood Pressure

Blood pressure is a product of the force with which your heart pushes blood through the blood vessels to get oxygen to all your tissues. Above-normal blood pressure increases the possibility of stroke and heart attack for two reasons. First, elevated blood pressure increases the tendency of the blood cells to clump together. Second, when a clump forms and a clot develops, it is pushed harder into the tiny vessel that it blocks. It follows that the higher the pressure, the harder the clot is forced into the blood vessel. Neither reason is good, but both together are bad, because they lead to more and larger clots.

Smoking can also raise blood pressure because the chemicals in smoke cause a slight constriction in blood vessels. This means the vessels give a stiffer-than-normal resistance to blood flow, so the heart responds with more force.

Because stroke and heart attack don't usually occur in young people, you might say, 'Look, I'm only 30 or 40 years old – do I really need to worry about this now?' My reply is 'Yes!' These risk factors accumulate with the years. But you don't realise it until you're sick. There are many things you can do to reduce blood clotting and keep blood pressure in line. By doing them you will keep your risk of stroke and heart attack near to the level of non-smokers. In fact, if you exercise too, you can probably bring your risk right down to 'average'.

As much as 23 per cent of the population have inherited a blood pressure problem. And it is more of a problem for anyone who smokes. Over the age of 60, about 75 per cent of us get high blood pressure. Since about 80 per cent of high blood pressure can be controlled completely by diet and lifestyle, everyone can take steps to bring their blood pressure into a normal range. Unfortunately, most people choose to control their blood pressure with drugs, making it a huge industry.

If your blood pressure is already high, you can bring it into line without relying on drugs. Chapter 7 explains how to reduce blood pressure with diet and exercise. If it is still normal, prevention is the best medicine for you. Start with vitamin-mineral balance, including calcium and magnesium, explained in Chapter 9, which will guard against osteoporosis. Dietary fibre also helps reduce blood pressure.

The major step to reduce platelet clumping, however, requires a change in intake of dietary oils. You may have heard of the omega-3 or fish oils. The name 'omega-3' refers to the basis of their chemical structure. All three of them have a unique structure at one end. This structure enables our body to use them in special ways.

Because their major source is fish, we call them fish or marine oils. Some plants provide them, as well.

Fish - A Brain Food

The omega-3 oils we get from fish are used in brain tissue and in specialised tissues in the eye's retina, which is really an extension of brain tissue. These same oils also help normalise blood platelet aggregation by reducing their tendency to clump. The omega-3 oils help to keep blood pressure in line in two ways. First, they reduce blood viscosity. Viscosity is a measure of the ease with which a fluid flows. High viscosity means it flows poorly, low viscosity means it flows easily. The higher the viscosity of the blood, the higher the blood pressure required to move it around. So if something helps blood viscosity, it also helps reduce blood pressure.

Secondly, one omega-3 oil is converted into a substance called prostaglandin PGE-3, which helps counter the tendency of nicotine to cause small blood vessels to tighten up. This tightening or constriction helps elevate blood pressure.

Omega-3 oils are also essential to the function of our immune system and in particular easing inflammation. The former effect accounts for their ability to reduce cancers, and the latter makes them important for treating and preventing rheumatoid arthritis, psoriasis and even migraine headache.

Fish oils, like most essential nutrients, start as plant oils that accumulate best in cold-water fish. Small fish and sea mammals, such as whales, eat cold-water algae and plankton containing an abundance of these marine oils. These oils are essential for fish and accumulate in their flesh because omega-3 oils don't solidify at deep ocean temperatures. Possibly they are also able to regulate pressure in the fish and mammals.

Where people have a diet high in fish or sea mammals rich in the omega-3 oils, rates of high blood pressure, stroke and heart attacks are much lower than in other parts of the world. In addition, inflammatory diseases such as rheumatoid arthritis are almost unknown. Omega-3 oils have been the subject of many clinical trials, and there is no question as to their value for human health.

The same oils are found in nuts, grasses and a few other plants. In the distant past, when the human diet consisted of venison, rabbit, goat and other free-range animals, we probably got much more of these oils from our diet than we do now. Nowadays we must take special care to include lots of fish in our menus and to use selected oils in cooking.

How Much Do You Need?

We're just beginning to understand the need non-smokers have for omega-3 oils, let alone smokers. But we can make an educated guess based on what we know. Dr Kristian S. Bierve of Denmark, an expert on human need for omega-3 oils, recommends that the average person strive for about one gram a day of omega-3 oils as an optimal level. We can speculate that doubling this amount would be both safe and prudent for smokers. Safe, because much higher doses (about ten times) have been tested on people with no unwanted effects, and prudent, because the need to reduce clumping in smokers is much higher than non-smokers. I believe that two grams is appropriate for smokers because their blood platelet aggregation is nearly double that of non-smokers.

Heart Disease Prevention – A Bonus

Heart disease develops through a complex sequence of events involving cholesterol and other blood fats. Smokers can reduce the risk of heart disease by increasing their use of antioxidants, but the omega-3 oils add a special bonus.

There are two general types of cholesterol, 'good' and 'bad'. The best way of measuring heart disease development is to monitor the ratio of total cholesterol to the 'good' or HDL cholesterol. HDL stands for high density lipoprotein, and this type of cholesterol will eventually be eliminated. Keeping the total cholesterol to HDL cholesterol ratio below 4 is ideal, along with keeping total cholesterol at 200 or less.

Omega-3 oils help push the ratio in the correct direction by helping the body make more 'good' cholesterol. Occasionally people who start using omega-3 oil supplements will find their total cholesterol increases. However, if they measure the ratio of total cholesterol to HDL cholesterol, they'll find that their risk has in fact decreased. What happens is that some 'bad' cholesterol is turned into good, and at the same time, more HDL cholesterol is also produced. So the total has increased, but the risk ratio has decreased.

Regular exercise is the most effective way to increase your 'good' cholesterol. More of that in Chapter 13. The best approach is to combine the use of omega-3 oils with exercise.

How Do I Get Omega-3 Oils?

We can make a three-pronged effort to increase our omega-3 oils by eating fish, cooking with the correct oils and using supplements.

TABLE 6.1 *Fish sources of omega-3 oils (per 3.5 oz. serving)*

Moderate *0.3–0.4 gram*	*High* *0.5–1.0 gram*
Bass	Anchovies
Catfish	Herring
Cod	Mackerel
Crustaceans (crab, lobster, shrimp)	Molluscs (clams, mussels, oysters, scallops, squid)
Halibut	Salmon
Perch	Swordfish
Snapper	Trout
Tuna	

Note: These values are relative. The best rule to follow is that the colder the water, the greater the omega-3 oil content. Fish rich in omega-3 oils usually are dark blue when viewed from the top.

TABLE 6.2 *Edible oils rich in omega-3 oils*

Cooking Oil	% Omega-3
Canola oil	10
Soybean oil	7

Supplemental Oils	% Omega-3
Cod liver oil	20
Linseed oil	57
Menhaden oil	23
Salmon oil	22

- Eat fish at least four times a week, and be sure to include fish high in omega-3 oils ('oily fish') at least twice.
- Cook and make salad dressings with soya bean oil.
- Add a tablespoon of linseed oil to your food daily, or take fish oil supplements.

Blood Pressure – Keeping it Down

High blood pressure is one of the most common health problems related to smoking. While research has never proved that smoking actually causes high blood pressure, it has proved that heightened blood pressure levels tend to return to normal when people stop smoking.

Smokers can do a lot to keep their blood pressure normal and to restore it to normal if it's not. If you're really serious about doing this, you MUST follow a complete dietary programme.

Taking Your Pulse

Find your pulse on the underside of your wrist. It's towards the outer edge if you are looking down while holding your palm upwards. Use the first three fingers of your left hand to find the pulse on your right wrist. Once you find your pulse, count it for a full minute. You're counting your heart-beat. Each beat forces blood through your arteries to every part of your body. Your pulse should be between 60 to 80 beats a minute.

Around 70 is average, but 60 or so is even better.

Experiment with your pulse. Take it when you're nervous, relaxed, after coffee, after a cigarette, after climbing the stairs, and get a general feeling for how it changes.

Blood Pressure

Your blood pressure can change similarly to your pulse rate. It is expressed as two numbers: diastolic and systolic. Systolic pressure is the pressure exerted when your heart beats and forces the blood through the arteries. Diastolic pressure is the remaining pressure between beats. Blood pressure is expressed as the ratio of these two numbers, with the systolic over diastolic pressure. Both numbers are in millimetres of mercury, and the systolic should be about 40 millimetres higher than the diastolic. If your systolic pressure is 105 and the diastolic (between-beat) pressure 65 (a healthy rate to have), it will be expressed as 105/65.

Blood pressure is measured with a device called a sphygmomanometer, which has three parts – a cuff, a sound detector and a pressure sensor. The cuff is hooked to a column of mercury which shows the pressure inside the cuff. The person checking your blood pressure listens with a stethoscope just below the cuff for Korotkoff sounds – named after the doctor who first identified them. To hear them it is necessary to release the cuff pressure slowly. At first, because the cuff is tight, nothing can be heard. As the pressure is released, there is a steady 'thumping' sound. This is the heart pushing blood past the cuff with each beat, and the pressure measured then is the systolic. The cuff pressure is allowed to fall just until the thumps are replaced by a steady 'whooshing' sound. Pressure at the instant the whoosh appears is the diastolic pressure.

I believe that a diastolic blood pressure of 85 and above is too high. When diastolic pressure reaches this reading regularly, it's time to take action. Systolic pressure rarely gets high by itself, but when it reaches 150 or more it's also too high.

TABLE 7.1 *Classification of high blood pressure*

Range in Millimetres of Mercury Diastolic BP	Category of High Blood Pressure
Less than 85	Normal
85 to 89	High normal
90 to 104	Mild hypertension
105 to 114	Moderate hypertension
115 or higher	Severe hypertension
Systolic BP with Diastolic	Category of High Blood Pressure
Less than 140	Normal
140 to 159	Borderline isolated systolic hypertension
160 or more	Isolated systolic hypertension

High blood pressure is called hypertension, and someone with hypertension is referred to as a hypertensive person. Hypertension is a 'silent killer' because most people don't know they have it until a doctor tells them. Its symptoms are so mild, and they usually develop so slowly, that it creeps up on you without you knowing it. It's one of the world's most insidious diseases, because it can cause someone to die from a stroke without even knowing there was a problem.

Two Types of High Blood Pressure

Secondary hypertension, as the name implies, is a side effect of some other illness. For example, adrenal tumours cause high blood pressure, pregnancy sometimes causes it, some kidney disorders and other conditions also cause hypertension. Once the cause is corrected, the blood pressure returns to normal. Secondary hypertension should be looked on as temporary and curable. Only about one to two percent of the population will ever get secondary hypertension, which accounts for about five per cent of the total number of cases of high blood pressure.

About 95 per cent of high blood pressure is called essential hypertension. It is caused by a number of environmental factors, including heredity, smoking, overweight, salt consumption, alcohol and other dietary factors. All these apart from heredity can be controlled. Heredity can predispose you to hypertension, but you can avoid it by controlling the other causes. It increases as people get older.

Eighty per cent of people can control their essential hypertension completely. Medication is necessary for only a minority of people. And many people can steadily decrease their medical drugs by using dietary measures in place of them.

Essential Hypertension – The Causes

Genetic programming inherited from our parents and grandparents governs much of what happens to us in life. However, some experts say that we also inherit the tendency to become alcoholics and drug addicts, yet most of us go through life without doing so because we decide to take control of ourselves. In fact, high blood pressure is just the same. Most people, though, have no idea of what they need to control in order to overcome it. Once you know the facts, it is no more necessary to submit to inherited tendencies regarding hypertension than it is addictions.

Overweight

Being overweight causes high blood pressure for two reasons. Extra fat means that the heart must pump harder to push blood through your capillaries. Pushing harder means higher blood pressure. So your heart works harder if you are overweight.

Being overweight increases blood pressure for a second, more complex reason. Extra fat makes some people produce more of the hormone insulin. Insulin is necessary for the body to use the blood sugar, glucose. It helps transport glucose into each cell of the body. Overweight people produce excess insulin because their extra fat cells require more of it than the fat cells of other people. And excess insulin causes the kidneys to raise the blood pressure. Smoking adds to this insulin effect, so an overweight smoker has two problems.

If overweight people with high blood pressure lose weight and follow a low-sugar, high-carbohydrate diet as described in this book (Chapter 14), their high blood pressure usually disappears completely.

Salt

Much high blood pressure is caused by too much salt. Salt upsets the ratio of potassium to sodium in the diet – the 'K factor'. Corn, for example has a K factor of 20 (219 milligrams of potassium and 11 milligrams of sodium), while cornflakes have a K factor of 0.07 (26 milligrams of potassium and 351 milligrams of sodium). Natural foods always have a K factor greater than three and usually above six, while processed foods are generally lower than one. See table 7.3 for more comparisons.

In the natural, unprocessed diet, salt is very scarce. In the Roman Empire soldiers were paid in a salt ration, much in the same way as early gold miners were paid in gold dust. The word 'salary' is derived from 'salt ration'. In a few isolated places in the world, salt still has this value.

When the dietary K factor of a group of people is

three or more, essential hypertension is very low – usually less than two per cent of the population – and mostly only very overweight people have it. As the ratio approaches one, however, high blood pressure in the population increases dramatically.

TABLE 7.2 *High blood pressure in a population*

K Factor	Population with High Blood Pressure (%)	Hypertension Origin
3.0 or more	2	Secondary
1.1	26	Essential
0.4	33	Essential

Don't get the idea that the K factor can be restored simply by increasing the amount of potassium in the diet. It can't, because the total amount of salt – specifically, sodium and chloride – must be taken into consideration. Most people with high blood pressure must control their sodium intake, salt consumption and K factor combined. I'll give some simple rules for doing this, but first some more explanation is necessary.

Sodium and potassium are the two major electrolytes in the body. A third electrolyte, chloride, is also essential. Electrolytes are minerals which are found in the body fluids and tissues. Potassium is very plentiful in natural food, so consuming it in correct amounts has never been a problem – until the present era of processed food. In contrast, sodium and chloride are very scarce in natural foods. Our kidneys not only eliminate waste materials, they're also designed to conserve sodium and chloride, because for about three million years of our existence these were very scarce. In a natural environment, conserving sodium and chloride would be one of the kidneys' most important functions. So not surprisingly, when there they find excess sodium and chloride – the two elements in common salt – the kidneys greedily conserve them. Through a complex series of interactions, this conservation of sodium and chloride causes an increase in blood volume, which produces high blood pressure. That's why we can't simply take potassium supplements to restore the balance and expect blood pressure to become normal.

About 50 per cent of hypertensive people are particularly sensitive to salt. These people cannot tolerate much more than about 300 milligrams of sodium daily, or about 500 milligrams of salt. By lowering their salt intake, they will be doing everything they can to improve their health. Their sodium/ potassium balance MUST be controlled.

Alcohol

Too much alcohol causes high blood pressure in most people, but some people are more sensitive to it than others. Alcohol makes high blood pressure worse for everyone, even if it's not the cause. And alcohol-related high blood pressure isn't helped by medicines. The message is clear: hypertensive people must use alcohol sparingly, if at all. Some people shouldn't consume any alcohol – and that means not even one drink! For others, one glass of wine, beer or mixed drink is the limit.

Type-A behaviour

Some people are by nature more tense and live lives of internally-generated stress. These are known as Type-A people, and they are more likely to have elevated blood pressure levels than more relaxed personalities. One way I use to tell if people have this kind of unrelaxed personality is to see if they finish other people's sentences. They can't wait for the other person to make their point – they must do it for them. If you find yourself doing this, take steps to reduce the internal stress you are generating.

External Stress

Stress is often generated externally, in the place of work, the home or in the environment where you live. It's practically impossible to eliminate external stress entirely, but if you don't take steps to reduce its impact, you can develop high blood pressure. The two approaches really work together: reducing it and reducing its effects on you. Dealing with stress does require strategic planning. There are plenty of books available dealing specifically with stress reduction techniques and I suggest you use them if you feel it is a problem. Also, follow the diet and supplement plans in this book and exercise every day. Daily exercise, preferably at the end of the day, eliminates the ravages of stress on the body better than any medicine ever can.

Essential Measures to Defeat High Blood Pressure

Reduce Salt Intake

Do not eat any food that provides over 75 milligrams of sodium, or any meal providing over 200 milligrams of sodium. It's not always easy to tell how much sodium is in the food you eat, but refer to nutritional labelling when available, or specialised nutritional tables. Try not to eat any food with added salt, whether home cooked or ready-prepared. Even if labels imply the product is low in salt, if any salt at all appears on the ingredient list, don't eat it. If you follow these rules, your diet will contain about 800 milligrams of sodium and less than 2,000 milligrams of salt daily. Some foods, such as milk, contain natural sodium. These foods are generally all right because they contain very little chloride. Natural sodium still adds up, but it's not as dangerous as sodium chloride and the body tolerates it better.

The Balanced K-Factor

Table 7.3 shows the sodium content, potassium content and the K factor of selected foods to illustrate how processing generally upsets the balance. A brief look at this table will show you why most processed food is out if you want to retain a balanced sodium: potassium ratio.

Let's look at the balance for beef. Most cuts provide about 44 milligrams of sodium and 311 milligrams of potassium – that's a K factor of around seven, which is excellent. But now do the same for a beef sausage. Even though it might have a high percentage of beef, it will also have a high salt content, which upsets its balance. Likewise, fresh sweetcorn is fine, but once it is processed into tinned corn (usually with added salt and sugar) or cornflakes, it changes entirely. However, there is one bright spot. Shredded Wheat is low in sodium and has an excellent K factor. Pasta, although not included on the list, is also good.

TABLE 7.3 *The nutritional cost of food processing (per serving)*

Food	Sodium (mg)	Potassium (mg)	K Factor
Beef	44	311	7.00
Chicken Breast	80	360	4.50
Corn (canned)	680	219	0.30
Corn (fresh)	11	219	20.00
Cornflakes	351	26	0.07
Fast food or frozen and breaded food	1,012	360	0.40
Hot dog (all beef)	461	71	0.15
Shredded Wheat	6	150	25.00

Omega-3 Fatty Acids

I call omega-3 oils 'nature's Teflon' when we are talking about blood pressure. These oils are found in the membranes of the cells that line blood capillaries and the blood cells themselves. They perform a simple but important function there: to make the arterial walls more slippery. They also make the membranes of the blood cells, especially red blood cells, more flexible. Because of this, the omega-3 oils actually make the blood flow more easily. Easier blood flow means the heart doesn't have to pump as hard to move the blood around. On a daily basis, I estimate that only about one to two grams of these oils is necessary if you eat a moderately low-fat diet. Follow the advice on preventing stroke discussed in Chapter 6.

Fat

Just as the correct oils help reduce blood pressure, incorrect fats can help to increase blood pressure. 'Incorrect' includes saturated fat. Processed meats are out, therefore, as well as high-fat cuts of meat. Eliminate the skin of poultry and stop using high-fat spreads. Not only do they contain the wrong kind of fat, they also give you excess salt.

Calcium–Magnesium

Research has demonstrated that extra calcium and magnesium can help clear high blood pressure, but usually only when people have intakes of these minerals far below the RNI of 700 mg a day for calcium and 300 mg for magnesium.

Water

Water helps your body flush out excess sodium and maintain correct fluid balance. Think of your body as a system of streams and rivers that are constantly bringing nutrients to your 50 trillion cells for nourishment. The entire system requires water and works more efficiently when it gets the water it needs.

Tap and bottled water, though, sometimes contain too much sodium. Labels on bottled waters should list the sodium content. You can find out the sodium content of your tap water from your local water authority. If the water contains less than 25 milligrams of sodium per quart, it is all right to drink. Remember too that you get water from other drinks, and from food, especially vegetables.

Fitness

Exercise will reduce blood pressure in most people all by itself. That's because most people are sedentary, and their vascular system is unfit. When they exercise, their blood vessels develop more flexibility, and their blood pressure drops a little. More flexible arteries and veins mean that when the heart beats, blood is forced not into a rigid set of pipes but into an elastic and yielding system. The result is that lower pressure is required to move the blood around. The arteries help the blood along rather than resisting its flow.

How much exercise is required to have an effect? Probably not as much as you may think. About 20 to 25 minutes of jogging daily, or 40 to 50 minutes of brisk walking. There are many variations that range from swimming, skiing, rowing or cycling, and a whole range of exercise machinery. They can all be interchanged. Chapter 13 gives you more information on exercise.

Eight Ways to Defeat High Blood Pressure

- Sodium: less than 800 mg daily
  No food over 75 mg
  No meal over 200 mg
  No salt substitutes
- K factor: at least 3, ideal is 5
  Eat natural foods
  No processed foods
  At least 3,000 mg of potassium daily
- Achieve ideal weight. Follow diet in Chapter 14
- Fibre: 30 grams minimum daily fibre supplement
- Water: Pure water, 32 fl oz per day minimum
- Basic supplements: Multivitamin, vitamins C, B complex, E
- Calcium–magnesium: 800 mg calcium, 400 mg magnesium daily
- Omega-3 oils: Fish and supplements giving 1,000 mg (one gram) daily

CHAPTER EIGHT

Cholesterol Control:
A Plan For Life

Smoking increases the rate of what is variously called heart disease, coronary heart disease, cardiovascular disease, atherosclerosis and hardening of the arteries. It all adds up to the same thing – smokers are more likely to die of a heart attack brought on by a blockage of one of the blood vessels in the heart. Blockage is the end result of a build-up of sludge, or plaque, that narrows these blood vessels so they can be blocked easily when an internal blood clot forms.

Smoking accelerates the accumulation of plaque in several ways. Materials in smoke irritate blood vessel linings and plaque is deposited as a protective substance. You can neutralise this irritant process by increasing your antioxidant reservoir (see Chapter 3).

For plaque to form, a type of cholesterol called low-density lipoprotein cholesterol, or LDL, must be present. We can look on this as 'bad' cholesterol. It is neutralised by 'good cholesterol' – high-density lipoprotein, or HDL. The risk of heart disease is related to the ratio (called the 'risk ratio') of total cholesterol to HDL ('good') cholesterol. This risk ratio should be

4 or less. Smoking increases the total cholesterol and decreases HDL cholesterol, thus increasing the risk ratio. The higher your risk ratio, the more plaque you will accumulate on your arteries. Thus, smoking increases the relative amount of bad cholesterol and decreases the amount of good cholesterol. I said 'relative' amounts because we want to lower total cholesterol and increase amounts of good cholesterol. If you do this consistently, smokers can reduce their risk of heart disease to below that of non-smokers.

Blood cholesterol levels are accepted worldwide as the best indicator of the rate at which plaque is aging the arteries. Lower your blood cholesterol, and keep it low, and you slow the aging of your arteries. Total blood cholesterol is easily and quickly measured, but a complete analysis of the several types of cholesterol and blood fats calls for about a tablespoon of blood and requires a specialised laboratory.

Measuring Cholesterol

Cholesterol is measured as so many milligrams per 100 millilitres (a decilitre) of blood. We can express it as milligrams per cent, but generally we simply state the number of milligrams of cholesterol. For example, I usually say my cholesterol is 190, even though there are really 190 milligrams in each decilitre. A range of between 180 to 220 is optimum. I recommend keeping 200 in mind as your target and aiming to get below it. Many scientists want us to strive for 175 or less. They also claim we have to increase good cholesterol.

If your cholesterol level goes above 240 and you smoke, you would do well to concern yourself about increasing your amount of 'good' cholesterol. We call HDL 'good' because it's cholesterol that's being swept from our arteries and taken out of the body through the excretory system. So it is best if the HDL part of the total cholesterol is as high as it can be. There seems to be an average upper limit for HDL of about 60 for men and 80 for women.

If you're a man whose cholesterol is 200 and you have an HDL of 55, that's very good. In contrast, if your total cholesterol is 250 and your HDL is still 55 (which is average), you have a higher risk of plaque development.

TABLE 8.1 *Cholesterol targets*

Total Cholesterol	*Heart Disease Risk*
175 mg/dl or lower	Low
200 mg/dl	Average
200–239 mg/dl	Above average
Over 240 mg/dl	High

Ratio of Total/HDL Cholesterol

Ratio	*Heart Disease Risk*
3.0 or less	Very low
3.5	Low
4.0	Below average
4.5	Average
5.0	Above average
6.0 or over	High
7.0 or over	Very high

Remember, too, that your cholesterol levels vary naturally from day to day, even from hour to hour, depending on diet, health and other factors. You can eliminate fluctuations by not eating for 12 hours before having your cholesterol measured – i.e. measuring it first thing in the morning. It's also better to have had a modest meal with no alcohol the night before.

Cholesterol also varies by five per cent with stress, exercise, sickness, smoking, health level and other factors.

- If your total cholesterol is consistently within five per cent of 200, keep doing what you are doing. Have your HDL measured and be sure it is enough to keep your ratio correct.
- If your total cholesterol is 175, congratulate yourself and keep your HDL high enough to have a low risk ratio.
- If your cholesterol is above 225 but your ratio of HDL good, you're still doing well. If it isn't, start a programme to lower your total cholesterol and raise HDL levels.
- If your cholesterol is 250 or above, take major steps to get your total cholesterol down and your HDL cholesterol up.

Why Cholesterol Levels Vary

About 80 per cent of the cholesterol in your blood was manufactured in your liver. Cholesterol performs certain important functions and is used as a raw material to make other body chemicals. So our body needs some cholesterol, and experts place the basic need between 125 and 150 milligrams.

Some cholesterol is converted to bile acids, which are essential for good digestion of fat or fatty materials. The gall bladder releases the bile acids through the bile duct into the small intestine just below the stomach. They combine with the food just after it leaves the stomach and help it mix completely.

Bile acids are natural detergents to help us digest fat by mixing it with water. If we don't get enough of the correct type of dietary fibre and some calcium, bile acids get reabsorbed further down the small intestine. Because the signals between reabsorbed bile acids and the liver are poor, the liver keeps making cholesterol and passes it into the blood instead of making more bile acids. So removing bile acids with fibre and calcium is the same as getting rid of cholesterol.

Blood Fat

When we eat saturated fat, it enters our bloodstream through a complex fat-circulation system called the lymphatic system. In the lymphatic system it forms into small droplets called chylomicrons. Cholesterol is essential to stabilise the fat that chylomicrons contain. Consequently, the more fat we eat, the more cholesterol we need in our blood. It's a natural fat stabiliser.

Experts keep advocating low-fat diets, because the more saturated fat we eat, the more cholesterol our livers must pump into our blood to maintain the right balance. Polyunsaturated fat (PUFA) – which is usually vegetable-derived – doesn't have to be stabilised as much. We can tolerate more of it without affecting our cholesterol levels.

Excess simple sugar – the kind you get in 'junk' foods – is converted to fat. Even though this fat is made in our body, it still requires cholesterol to be stabilised, because it enters our blood. That's why people who eat too much sugar also have raised cholesterol levels. The moral is: keep both fat and sugar intake to a minimum.

Men Only – The Abdominal Paunch

Excess weight raises cholesterol levels in both men and women. However, men have a special problem with abdominal fat. Many men develop a 'paunch' in middle age, and even a small one is enough to raise cholesterol. Abdominal fat seems to send a message to the liver saying: 'produce more cholesterol'. Smoking increases the tendency to more abdominal fat. While a flat stomach looks good, it is also healthy. So smokers must watch their diet and exercise. Sit-ups and exercises that produce strong abdominal muscles and reduce abdominal fat are especially useful to combat abdominal paunches.

Lowering Total Cholesterol

- Increase dietary fibre. Soluble fibre supplements help lower cholesterol.

- Reduce total dietary fat, especially saturated fat. This means cutting down on animal foods and increasing low-fat foods. Become more of a vegetarian – but watch out for hard cheeses and dairy products, which also have high fat content.
- Reduce refined sugar consumption. Eat carbo-hydrates in the form of vegetables, fruit, natural fruit juice, and wholegrain foods. These can include cereals, pasta, breads.
- Make sure your weight and abdominal measurement are what they should be. Men should have a waist-to-hips ratio of 0.9 and women 0.8. This ratio is taken by measuring your waist and your hips, where you feel your bones, and dividing your waist measurement by that of your hips. As it exceeds these numbers, cholesterol creeps up.

Raising HDL Cholesterol

You can also reduce your overall risk of heart disease by increasing your HDL (good) cholesterol. If you raise good cholesterol whilst lowering total cholesterol, you gain a whole new lease of life. You reduce your total risk by 7 per cent for every point you elevate your HDL above 45. For example: a total cholesterol of 200 and an HDL of 44 yields a risk ratio of 4.5, which is good. Now consider a total cholesterol of 200 and an HDL of 50 which gives a risk ratio of 4 – excellent. A small increase in HDL produces a significant risk reduction.

HDL is raised by regular aerobic exercise such as brisk walking for 40 minutes, or jogging, cycling or swimming for 20 minutes. Other forms of aerobic exercise such as skipping with a rope work as well (see Chapter 13).

You can also raise your HDL by increasing your polyunsaturated (vegetable) oil intake and also your omega-3 oils. This means eating lot of dark-skinned fish, such as salmon, mackerel and tuna, and using an omega-3 oil supplement (see Chapter 6). HDL cholesterol also increases when you consume enough soluble fibre. While soluble fibre decreases total cholesterol, it helps elevate good cholesterol.

Putting It Into Practice

In essence, then, you need to use a soluble fibre supplement while increasing dietary fibre, to lose weight if necessary and to reduce total fat and saturated fats while increasing polyunsaturated and omega-3 oils. Let's see how this might work in practice.

Increased fibre: To consume enough fibre, we must eat a wholegrain cereal without added sugar, also daily fruit and vegetables, and wholegrains. Even if you do nothing else, take a soluble-fibre supplement daily. This will reduce cholesterol. The best type is psyllium husk. It will help eliminate bile acids, dietary cholesterol and fat. Even people who eat a balanced diet don't usually get enough of these soluble fibres. When three to five grams of a soluble fibre supplement are taken three times daily (with meals), cholesterol levels usually fall by ten to 25 per cent in one to three months. Stick with it regularly, and be patient. Your cholesterol got high over many years, so give it time to come down.

Reduce total fat: Avoid processed and red meat, and choose low- fat dairy products. Eat fish and poultry and vegetarian meals of pasta, beans and wholegrains.

Lower saturated fat: Most saturated fats are obtained from red meat, processed meats, and high fat dairy products, also commercially deep-fat fried foods. So, don't eat:

- Red meat, including beef, pork, lamb, more than once weekly.
- Processed meat of any type, including those made from turkey or chicken.
- Organ meat, including liver, kidney, brains, heart, stomach and the like.
- Poultry skin
- Fried foods, including deep-fat fried fish.
- High-fat dairy products, including milk, butter, cheese, ice cream and whole-milk yoghurts.

Do eat:

- White meat or poultry with skin removed.
- Fish, including shellfish four times weekly or more.
- Low-fat dairy products including yoghurt, cottage and ricotta cheeses.
- Corn oil or margarine.

Reduce refined sugar: Avoid highly processed foods, especially those containing sugar and syrups. Avoid sweet desserts and cakes. Learn to enjoy fruit, if you don't already.

Control your weight: Excess body weight is the simple result of too many calories coming in as food and not enough going out as exercise. Diet naturally by taking in fruit, vegetables, grains, and beans which provide satisfying meals without overloading on the calories. Burn more calories by establishing regular exercise habits. Exercise will also help turn fat into muscle and turn abdominal paunches into flat stomachs.

Niacin - An Aggressive Cholesterol-Lowering Approach

Studies have shown that niacin, one of the B vitamins, can profoundly lower cholesterol and reduce heart disease risk. Niacin can bring about several important changes:

- It reduces triglycerides which work in tandem with LDL cholesterol.
- It raises HDL cholesterol.
- It lowers total cholesterol.

So if you add niacin to your diet, you will reduce your heart disease risk even more. That's the good news. The bad news is that niacin can have some side effects, such as flushing of the face, nausea and skin irritation, which can be uncomfortable but not serious. The RNI for niacin is 16 or 17 mg a day for men (lower as you get older), and 12 or 13 mg a day for women. However, some United States research shows that it is possible to take from 250 mg to one gram a day, creating a ten per cent reduction of total cholesterol and similar elevation of HDL cholesterol with no noticeable side effects. It takes about six months for the effects of niacin to emerge fully.

Drug Treatment

A number of prescription drugs are given routinely to lower cholesterol and raise HDL cholesterol. They are resins which act like a type of super-fibre and are generally used when dietary measures are not having any effect or when total cholesterol is over 300. They may be a useful short-term measure, but it is always advisable to use all other methods at your disposal together with them and in the hope of eventually eliminating them.

CHAPTER NINE

Building Strong Bones

All women risk developing osteoporosis as they age. Women who smoke or live with a smoker have a much higher than average risk of the disease. Osteoporosis means exactly what its name implies: osteo = bones, porosis = porous. Osteoporosis, which is accelerated by smoking, is another of those insidious diseases that sneak up on us over about 25 years or more, and then emerge as a serious disorder. Osteoporosis affects most women, but very few men. Prevention of osteoporosis is not just the best medicine – it's the only medicine.

The Development of Porous Bones

Osteoporosis is a disease in which the bones lose calcium and become porous. A normal bone is hard and dense, like a solid plastic block, while an osteoporotic bone is spongy, light and very brittle.

Calcium is a dynamic bone mineral. Your blood calcium is always about ten milligrams per 100 millilitres of blood, give or take a milligram or so. In lay terms, it's often referred to as 10 milligrams per cent, or simply 'a calcium count of ten'. People always lose some calcium in urine, sweat and stools, even if they aren't getting any more calcium from their diet. It's rather like a bank account where there's always some cash going out, whether or not any is coming in. However, even under conditions of all loss and no gain – called 'negative calcium balance' – a person's blood calcium level would always remain at around ten milligrams percent. How come it stays the same if you take in no calcium, and lose some daily?

Simple. People have a huge calcium reservoir in the body, in the form of bones. If you get more calcium than you lose – that is, maintain a positive calcium balance – and do other things right, such as exercise, your bones build up and stay dense. If you excrete more calcium than you take in through your diet, your bones start to lose out. That's why we say calcium is dynamic, because it's constantly coming and going, although the blood level remains practically constant. A departure from the normal level of blood calcium is serious.

Most young women stop getting enough dietary calcium from around the age of 15. This means they are in a state of negative calcium balance. The deficit is usually so small it goes unnoticed. The backbone is probably most vulnerable to the loss, but other bones – such as the hips, ankles and lower jawbone – are at risk too, in that order. The backbone and the bone on which the bottom teeth rest are naturally spongy, shock-absorbing bones, and this predisposes them to losing their calcium first. Living in a metropolitan area with unclean air also induces calcium loss – as does smoking.

As the menopause approaches, a woman's supply of oestrogen slows down. Oestrogen – a hormone needed for the reproductive process – is also needed to activate bone cells that deposit calcium. Once women go through the menopause and oestrogen production slows to a trickle or stops completely, bone loss accelerates unless they take in enough dietary calcium and exercise consistently.

Extra oestrogen (in the form of HRT, hormone replacement therapy) is often prescribed when a woman faces definite bone loss. It can also be given simply if the woman is in a high risk category, such as a smoker, if she has a family history of osteoporosis, and also if she is of a genetic type which predisposes her to the disease – i.e. small and bony, with light skin and eyes.

Women who smoke, or are passive smokers, don't produce as much oestrogen as non-smoking women. This nicotine-induced oestrogen decline slows bone building even where there is adequate calcium intake, and accelerates bone loss where there is not. But because bones represent such a large reservoir of calcium, you won't notice the depletion process.

Let's look at the mathematics of this. If you had a loss of five milligrams of calcium a day, starting at age 20, that would come to 350 grams of calcium lost by the age of 40. That's just over three-quarters of a pound. A women who weighs around nine stone at the age of 40 should have about five pounds of calcium in her bones. If she has lost three-quarters of a pound, she is 15 per cent short. Yet all those years her blood calcium level has stayed at 10 milligrams per cent. This shortage in her bones won't show up except by very sophisticated bone density tests.

As the woman goes through the menopause at between the age of 45 and 55, oestrogen production slows down and the calcium loss accelerates. Since the backbone gives up its calcium first, her shoulders may start to round a little, and she could notice some low-back pain. As the bone loss continues, she will gradually become shorter. If the calcium loss is severe, she could develop crushed vertebrae in the back and by age 65 or 70 may be as much as six inches shorter than she was at the age of 30. There may also be the rounding of the upper back that we call 'dowager's hump'. Also, since osteoporotic bones are more fragile than solid bones, they shatter like glass when they are broken instead of like a stick, thus leading to more difficult fractures. We used to accept all this as an inevitable part of aging, but we now know it is possible to prevent the worst effects of this process.

Building and Keeping Dense Bones

First you've got to get enough calcium. The RNI says 700 mg per day, but I recommend at least 1,000 mg per day for all women past the teenage years. Some experts even argue in favour of 1,200 or even 2,000 milligrams daily. The reason you need this much calcium is because your body only absorbs about 40 per cent of your actual calcium intake, no matter what form it's in. But nature doesn't waste the extra calcium, because it plays a role in reducing heart disease and the risk of colonic cancer.

A smoker should strive for 1,200 milligrams of calcium a day. 1,500 milligrams is even better. Regular weight-bearing exercise makes dietary calcium even more effective. We'll talk about exercise later on in this chapter and again in Chapter 13. Magnesium is also essential for good health and seldom gets the recognition it deserves. It works closely with calcium and is found in many of the same foods. You should get around 400 mg of magnesium daily.

TABLE 9.1 *Practical calcium food sources*

Food	Serving	Food Calcium	Servings for 1,000 mg
Sardines, with bones	3 oz.	372	2.6
2% milk	1 cup	352	2.8
Skim milk	1 cup	296	3.4
Yogurt (low-fat)	1 cup	272	3.7
Oysters	¾ cup	170	5.9
Canned salmon, with bones	3 oz.	167	6.0
Spinach	½ cup	106	9.4
Creamed cottage cheese	¼ cup	58	17.3
Broccoli	½ cup	49	20.0
Beans	½ cup	45	22.0

Table 9.1 lists the best sources of calcium. You'll see that your diet is unlikely to give you enough calcium unless you like dairy foods, because they are particularly calcium-rich. Some plant sources of calcium aren't all

that useful because they contain acids which make the calcium difficult for the body to use. Look at the number of servings necessary to obtain 1,000 milligrams of calcium and you'll realise that low-fat dairy products are essential if you don't want to use supplements.

I've also listed the ingredients of an ideal calcium supplement. Notice that this supplement contains magnesium, which is essential for energy, bone development, maintaining normal blood pressure and good nerve function.

Your diet plus a good multi-vitamin and multi-mineral supplement should provide from 800 to 1,000 milligrams of calcium daily. By using an extra calcium supplement, you could raise your daily calcium intake to 2,000 milligrams.

Exercise and Bone

'If you don't use it, you lose it' is an old saying that applies to everything we have, but especially to our bones. It takes energy for your body to maintain strong, dense bones. Consequently, if you don't use your bones, your brain's primitive logic says 'Relax, you can afford to let go of some of that calcium.' Exercise sends a counter-signal to the brain saying, 'Look at all this work I'm doing. I need the bones.' The body must expend energy to maintain strong bones. If we don't use them regularly, they simply lose calcium and become weak.

Which exercise, and how often? Weight-bearing exercise – which you would be best to do at your local gym, and under supervision at first – is ideally done three or four times a week. A brisk walk while carrying small hand weights is less strenuous and also helpful. The important thing is to walk for at least 30 minutes – longer if possible. Carrying and swinging the hand weights keeps your arm and hand bones strong. If you squeeze down on the weights, it helps your forearm bones as well.

Good daily exercise also includes the following: jogging (20 to 30 minutes), skipping with a rope (20 minutes), cycling (30 to 60 minutes), an aerobic workout (30 minutes high impact, 50 minutes low impact). Swimming, although not a weight bearing exercise, is also good if you do laps and maintain a brisk pace for 30 minutes or more. Playing around in the water won't work!

Do I Need Oestrogen Supplements?

Doctors are increasingly advocating hormone replacement for women, although the subject is still controversial. If you are leading the ideal lifestyle, eating and exercising well and not suffering undue stress, your body should be able to cope with the menopause in a natural way so that its effects are minimal. Do not be bludgeoned by medical science into taking a hormonal supplement, but if you feel that your oestrogen loss is making life a misery – and you have osteoporotic tendencies – there could be a case for treatment. Remember though that the long-term effects of hormone replacement are not proven, and there is some evidence that it increases the risk of breast cancer. Any therapy, traditional or controversial, should be based on accurate bone-density measurements. Clinical studies on women up to 106 years of age have proven unequivocally that maintaining and increasing bone density requires calcium and exercise.

Childbirth

Although I would strongly advise every woman to give up smoking during pregnancy, if you absolutely can't you should take extra calcium to protect yourself and your child. Chapter 10 focuses on protecting the baby, so here I'll talk about the mother's bones.

Childbirth extracts an added burden on the mother's bone reserves because her body is called upon to produce a second skeleton. If the mother doesn't get enough calcium, nature takes it from her bones, thus increasing her risk of osteoporosis and also the likelihood of a smaller-than-normal baby. Recent research suggests that when dietary calcium doesn't meet the extra demand, the shortage causes high blood pressure, often in the later stage of pregnancy. This high blood pressure can be dangerous for you and for the baby, so don't let it happen.

There's only one solution – take more calcium. I

recommend 2,000 milligrams daily (the RNI says an extra 550 mg per day on top of the 700 mg required for non-pregnant women). The most practical solution is a good calcium-magnesium supplement.

Will All That Calcium Constipate Me?

When people start taking calcium, they often think they're becoming constipated. In fact, their stools are becoming more dense because about 60 per cent of the calcium is excreted. However, remember what I said about fibre? If you get all the fibre you need, there will be no problem with constipation.

Advice to Men

Osteoporosis rarely affects men, for several reasons. Men consume more calcium and tend to satisfy their RNI for calcium for longer than women, until they're well into their 20s. Women tend to diet and watch their figures starting as teenagers, and so cut down or omit altogether high-fat foods which also means they miss out on the calcium contained in them, especially dairy produce. Men also do more weight-bearing exercise longer into their adult life. Another plus for them is that they don't bear children and don't experience the menopause.

Consequently, men don't begin experiencing a decline in bone density until well into their mid-30s and even early 40s. Because there's no menopause to accelerate the loss in bone mass, the decline is slow but it is steady. The longer men live, the greater their probability of osteoporosis – especially if they smoke, drink coffee and eat meat.

Not surprisingly, older men are showing the signs of osteoporosis. Though the numbers don't come anywhere near the statistics of women, it nonetheless is possible that men will routinely have osteoporosis unless they too take preventative steps. The same rules apply to men as to women. Calcium and exercise are the keys to osteoporosis prevention. Indeed, there's no therapy once the disease has begun – only prevention. So when I say women who smoke should get 1,200 milligrams of calcium and daily exercise, the same advice is prudent for men too.

CHAPTER TEN

Smoker's Skin – Avoiding the Ravages

We can make our skin look more healthy and beautiful from the outside with creams, oils and other toiletries. However, what goes on inside the body, as a result of diet and lifestyle, has a more dramatic and lasting effect on skin tone. Even if you smoke, eating the right food and choosing the correct lifestyle will help your skin become supple and develop a healthy glow.

Skin is your body's largest organ. It's about six per cent of your total body weight and covers a large area. For example, a nine-stone, five foot five inch woman has over 16 square feet of skin weighing over seven pounds. A six foot two inch, 14-stone man has over 21 square feet of skin weighing over 14 pounds. The lungs and small intestines have large surface areas but not the proportionate weight.

Like all organs and tissues, the skin is made up of countless cells arranged in two major layers. The epidermis, the outer layer of the skin, consists of two layers: an outer layer of dead cells (the stratum corium) and a lower layer of live cells. Below the live layer of epidermis is the dermis. The dermis is a live, vital tissue filled with small blood vessels, sweat glands, nerves and other microscopic organs essential to the maintenance of the skin. Skin cells in the epidermis reproduce every three to six weeks, depending on your health, nutrition, and heredity. These cells reproduce from the bottom, so each new cell pushes the old one upwards. As the old cells progress upward, they move further from the vital, life-giving nutrients, including oxygen, in the dermis, and they can't eliminate their wastes, so they die. This progression means that the outer layer of the epidermis consists entirely of dead, dehydrated, flattened cells. They are made mostly of protein, pigments, some oils and carbohydrate, and they slough off when we wash and scrape our skin against clothing.

Follicles from which hairs grow are actually appendages of the epidermis that extend deep inside the dermis. By residing deep in the dermis, and even into the tissue below the dermis, hair follicles are well nourished by blood vessels. These hair follicles produce cells that die and become part of the hair shaft.

Sweat glands, which originate in the dermis, are connected to the surface by tiny openings called pores. A pore often has a hair growing out of it, and the opening serves two purposes. One is an opening for the hair, the other permits water to be released. Sweat glands go deep into the dermis where they produce water for excretion at the surface. When this surface water evaporates, it removes body heat that helps keep your body cool in the summer and when you're working or exercising.

Sebaceous glands are often associated with the hair

follicle. These glands produce oils that give the hair its sheen and make the dry epidermal cells more soft and supple. These oils also help protect our skin from the sun, dry air, harsh chemicals and other environmental effects.

The network of blood capillaries in the dermis supplies the most important nutrient, oxygen, and removes the most important waste, carbon dioxide. These capillaries also transport everything that gets into your blood. If you smoke, they transport nicotine and some pigments from smoke. Consequently, sensitive people can smell the smoke in your skin just as they can smell garlic on your breath.

The Skin's Responsibilities

Skin shields you from the sun, chemicals, bacteria, and countless environmental factors. It's waterproof so you don't swell up when caught in the rain or dry out when in the hot sun. At the base of the dermis, a layer of fat serves as a shock absorber to protect your internal organs, insulate them from the cold, and keep in body heat.

A marvellous network of nerves in the dermis, connected to the hair follicles, can simultaneously detect the slightest touch, temperature change, air flow and even changes in barometric pressure. These same nerves sense environmental changes inside and outside your body. Your body then adjusts blood flow to either conserve or dissipate heat. When it needs to dissipate heat, the capillaries let blood flow to the skin, the sweat glands go into action producing water for evaporation, and heat is given off. Conversely, when it's cold out or you need to conserve body heat, the capillaries tighten and the skin doesn't get as much blood. Because the insulating fat layer is below the dermis, this marvellous system works independently to control body heat.

Changes in our hormones profoundly affect the skin. So do drugs and food. So caffeine, nicotine, alcohol and our emotions cause changes in the skin. In this way the skin reflects our mood and lets those around us know if we're tense, relaxed or simply feeling good.

Natural Skin Pigment

Skin pigment and thickness evolved from human survival needs. With the need to modulate sunlight there developed differentiation in colour, dryness, thickness and oiliness. These tendencies are no longer so important because we can spend our lives in regulated environments, but inherited factors still make skins different. Natives of equatorial areas between the Tropics of Cancer and Capricorn have thick, dark, sometimes absolutely black skin to prevent the sun's rays from penetrating it. In contrast, Northern people, from places like Iceland or Lapland, tend to have thin, light skin which will trap the weak sun rays of these regions. People who live in the temperate zones in between those extremes have the ability to produce pigment that filters sunlight. They tan if exposed gradually to sunlight.

Dark skin tends to be oily to keep moisture in and sunlight out. Light skin is non-oily and dry, allowing sunlight to pass through.

Skin and hair colour are usually co-ordinated. Blue eyes are more sensitive for lower northern light levels, and light hair is more easily seen in the dark. Consistent with light skin, light hair is thin, not dense, and contains little pigment. Dark eyes are less sensitive to the harsh light of equatorial regions.

This can help you understand why light skin, hair and eyes are more sensitive to smoke and fumes than darker skin, hair and eyes. Light skin is more sensitive because it is thinner and has less protective oil and pigments, so irritants can penetrate more easily.

Smoking and Skin Colour

Smokers are often noted for having grey skin and thin hair. Some people have claimed that smoking darkens the hair. This is consistent with the effect of tobacco tars and nicotine on the skin. Light skinned people are more affected by smoking and dark skinned people less so.

Let's see how the skin can take on colour. If you eat enough carrots, carrot juice or beta carotene, you'll turn orange, because beta carotene accumulates in the epidermal cells. At one time a yellowish carotenoid pigment, canthaxanthine, was sold as a way of getting a tan, but it was withdrawn because it was not within safety guidelines.

The movement of carotenoid pigments from the dermis to the epidermal cells is a healthy measure, because they modulate sunlight and help protect the skin. Enough beta carotene will help prevent burning and produce a good tan.

Pigments in tobacco that are carried in tobacco smoke have similarities to beta carotene, canthaxanthine and other plant pigments. After these pigments are breathed into the lungs, some pass into the blood. Once they enter the blood, they eventually find their way into the epidermis. If you smoke enough, one reason your skin will appear grey is because it is burdened with dark pigments found in tobacco smoke.

A second reason why your skin appears grey is because nicotine causes the capillaries of the epidermis to become constricted. Constricted capillaries do not supply the dermis and epidermis with as many nutrients, especially oxygen. The result is the absence of the healthy glow of normal skin, because the cells are being deprived of the natural pigments in blood.

Strategy for Better Coloured Skin

You can return to a healthy glow by restoring better nutrition and by supplying the correct plant pigment and lots of oxygen to build a healthy dermis and epidermis. This means following the advice for getting enough antioxidants, the diet strategy in Chapter 14, and the exercise programme in Chapter 13. Let's review what each step accomplishes.

In Chapter 14 you will be introduced to a diet rich in protein, low in fat and with the correct carbohydrate ratio. A supplement plan to supply more beta carotene is also provided. Follow this plan and you will get a variety of carotenoid pigments, including beta carotene, canthaxanthine, lycopene, and many others. In addition, you'll get all types of dietary fibre. This will keep you regular and also help eliminate tobacco pigments from your body.

By taking supplements of beta carotene, you will supply your skin with pigments that help make your skin glow. If you are a heavy smoker or have light skin, take more beta carotene for added protection and better skin colour. It will take three to six weeks for the plan to start showing results, so a little patience is required.

Exercise will improve your circulation. It increases metabolism, moves more blood to the body surface, and gets more oxygen to the cells in the epidermis. This increased metabolism speeds skin turnover and eliminates dead cells more rapidly. There is no substitute for exercise!

Exercise and B vitamins go together. Both together enhance the effects of each other, increasing circulation, improving skin metabolism and helping incorporate the carotenoid pigments into the skin cells.

Skin and Hair Condition

Smoking is hardest on light skin because it shows colour better, is thinner and less hydrated. Omega-3 oils and vitamin E can help. Both these nutrients will increase the surface oils by adding oils to the epidermis via the dermis and the sebaceous glands. Also, vitamin E keeps the omega-3 oils from being damaged by the oxidising materials in tobacco smoke. If you've got light, dry skin and you smoke, you're likely to have thin, listless hair. Hair is produced by a group of specialised epidermal cells in an appendage of the epidermis, which goes down into the dermis, where it is bathed with blood and the nutrients contained in it.

So, by supplementing your diet and exercising, you improve the internal quality of each hair. It's a natural outcome of better nutrition. However, there's more you can do to add a nice sheen to your hair – supplement your diet with omega-3 oils.

Each hair has a small gland alongside it called a sebaceous gland. As each hair grows outwards, it becomes coated with the oil produced by the sebaceous gland. This coating gives lustre and sheen to the hair. Adding omega-3 oils, vitamin E and beta carotene to your supplement programme increases the output of your sebaceous glands. The result is not only supple, healthy-looking skin, but better hair quality as well.

When Do I Get Results?

Improving the skin is a slow process. You need to keep your programme going for at least four weeks before you will start to notice a difference. The longer you've been smoking, the longer it will take to improve your skin because you've got more pigments to get rid of. Perseverance is required, but will definitely pay off.

Better hair calls for even more patience. Hair grows about one-third of an inch to one inch a month. Consequently, if you start today and have average hair growth, you won't notice the results for about three months. But as with skin, the results are worth it.

Will Protein Help?

Most people, smokers included, get plenty of protein. However, if you want to make an added effort, a little extra protein will improve skin and hair growth. You can add protein to your diet with a protein supplement. Or you can just add an extra egg to your daily diet. Because you'll be eating more fibre and using a fibre supplement, the added cholesterol won't hurt. In addition, the oils in the egg yolk will improve the sheen of your hair.

Putting It Together

Table 10.1 sums up the steps you can take to improve skin colour and tone and hair condition.

You've probably noticed by now that many of the preventative measures I've described are somewhat repetitious. For example, you can take antioxidants to prevent heart disease, cancer, cataracts and emphysema. The omega-3 oils help prevent heart attack and stroke. More, exercise helps all of these and even improves skin and hair colour. These improvements happen because the same nutrients and antioxidants have beneficial effects on all tissues.

TABLE 10.1 *Skin and hair improvement*

- Antioxidant supplements: beta carotene, vitamin E and selenium, vitamin C.
- Stress-fighter vitamins: B vitamins, including all the B vitamins, with at least 100 per cent of the U.S. RDA.
- Omega-3 oils: 1 gram daily (usually three capsules).
- Optional protein supplement; take about 15 grams daily. Or eat an egg daily.
- Diet: follow the Smoker's Longevity Diet in Chapter 14.
- Exercise: five days weekly for at least twenty minutes at a training heart rate.

Avoiding the Wrinkles

Scientific research now confirms that smokers have more wrinkles than non-smokers. How can something you do with your lungs create such an effect on your skin?

Some researchers say it's because smokers squint more, due to the irritation of smoke on the eyes. Squinting produces wrinkles if you do it long enough. Biochemists, in contrast, look at the protein – collagen – that holds skin together. They say this protein is damaged indirectly by materials in smoke. Both are contributory factors, although I believe the collagen theory is more viable.

Collagen is often called 'nature's nylon'. It is a protein

that forms a matrix of fibres throughout the dermis and the fatty tissue, or subcutaneous fat, just below the dermis. Like nylon, collagen is woven into a net-like structure that has multi-directional strength.

However, nylon is a homogeneous man-made fibre that looks the same everywhere. Collagen is not. Like all proteins, collagen consists of about 22 'building blocks' called amino acids. These are linked together into small fibres, which are intertwined with each other until a large fibre is built. Then the large fibres intertwine.

Collagen, like everything in the body, is in a state of dynamic equilibrium. That means it is being broken down and rebuilt constantly. Like skin, which is replenished on average every three weeks when we're young and every six to eight weeks as we get older, collagen is renewed regularly. And, as when any protein is re-made, something can go wrong.

For the body to build collagen or any other material, it needs energy, raw materials, vitamins and minerals. Generally energy is available in the form of blood sugar. Basic materials are available if you eat a reasonably good diet. But several critical nutrients, such as vitamin C and some B vitamins needed to make collagen, are destroyed by smoking.

As I've mentioned before, oxygen can be lacking in a smoker's blood. In addition, skin is an external tissue and smoking tends to cause peripheral tissue capillaries to tighten. Thus there are two reasons smokers may not have enough oxygen, an essential nutrient in energy production. In previous chapters an exercise and iron-supplement programme was recommended to make up for that shortage.

Once you've got the energy and the amino-acid building blocks, you need several vitamins, including vitamin C, some B vitamins and the minerals zinc and magnesium. You've seen several reasons why these are likely to be in short supply for smokers. Smokers' diets are often short in vitamins and minerals to begin with. And smoking destroys vitamin C and some B vitamins. It also imposes a greater need for other antioxidant nutrients.

You know that getting plenty of antioxidants is the most efficient way to make up for this dietary shortfall and antioxidant destruction. Take at least 500 mg of vitamin C daily and up to 2,000 mg (two grams) if you want extra insurance. Take beta carotene, vitamin E and balanced B-complex supplements daily. The diet in Chapter 14 will provide the necessary minerals, as will using a balanced vitamin–mineral food supplement and the calcium–magnesium supplement described in Chapter 9.

Collagen Injections

Cosmetic surgery has made major advances in recent years. Collagen injections are a relatively new technique which may be useful in the short term. Collagen is injected into the area of a wrinkle to fill the void that exists. The wrinkle disappears and the skin looks smooth and supple. Anyone wishing to use this technique must go to an approved cosmetic surgeon.

Collagen injections last for six to 12 months and then have to be renewed. A course is expensive and the impermanence of the technique is another minus factor. Prevention is still the best cure.

Squinting and Your Skin

If collagen is constantly being removed and replaced, why do wrinkles develop in the first place? That's where the 'squinting' hypothesis comes in.

When you squint a wrinkle develops. In the small area where the skin folds, the cells and tissue are squeezed. Though it's not the same as severely restricting blood flow in your leg, for instance, where you might get cramp and tingling, squinting does restrict blood flow and nutrients. Collagen synthesis doesn't take place at that spot for however long you keep squinting, even if it's only an instant. If you stop collagen synthesis for an instant it doesn't matter. But do it regularly for a day, many times a day, and it does. In fact, cell reproduction in the area declines and a wrinkle, or crease, develops.

A good comparison are the depressions or 'pockmarks' often left from adolescent acne. The difference is that acne causes a loss of collagen and death to the cells in the area because of the localised infection that cause it in the first place. The area is depressed because of missing tissue.

One good way to prevent wrinkle development is to

practise not squinting. Smoke in areas where the smoke is blown away, so you won't have to squint or frown so much.

Exercise Prevents Wrinkles Too

Exercise increases blood flow to your skin by at least 100 per cent. If you exercise actively enough, your skin temperature will increase by a couple of degrees. Although this increase doesn't seem like much, the rate of metabolism and the building and renewing of body tissue, including the skin, increases by over 35 per cent.

Besides this, exercise stimulates your body's production of a group of natural steroids we call anabolic steroids. Anabolism is the building of new tissue. These anabolic steroids actually stimulate protein synthesis. It's why regular work-outs increase muscle mass and strength. They also build healthy skin.

Omega-3s Again

In Chapter 6 and 7 I explored the need for omega-3 oils in helping you prevent strokes and heart attacks. They will help you look better, too. Briefly, the omega-3 oils, specifically one called EPA, help relax the blood capillaries. Think of them as countering, to some extent, the action of nicotine on the blood vessels. By following the dietary programme in Chapter 14 and taking about one gram of omega-3 oils daily, you'll be taking a giant step in wrinkle prevention.

Gums and Teeth

Smoking affects gum tissue much as it works on the skin. Gum tissue is a marvel of collagen and saliva production, organised to anchor and protect the teeth.

Teeth are anchored to the underlying bone with specialised collagen fibres. Though gum tissue doesn't wrinkle, a more insidious process takes place.

If gum tissue isn't kept strong and healthy, bacteria can grow in the area where teeth and gums meet. These bacteria can slowly destroy the collagen fibres. We call this periodontal disease. 'Peri' means around, and 'odontin' means teeth – literally, a disease around the teeth.

Periodontal disease gives an early warning called gingivitis, characterised by bleeding gums. This is not something that should be dismissed just because it doesn't hurt or seems to pass quickly.

Research has shown that gingivitis cleared up when patients regularly took 600 mg of vitamin C. This should come as no surprise, because we know that vitamin C is essential for collagen production. And the basic cause of gingivitis is unhealthy collagen.

However, smokers have a higher incidence of gingivitis. Since smoking affects nutrient delivery to all tissues and destroys vitamin C, it follows that smokers with gingivitis require more than 600 mg.

The real solution for gingivitis is the prevention of gum disease. It lies in all the measures we've taken to produce healthy skin – the exercise, dietary and supplement plans will help create healthy gums along with fewer wrinkles.

Leathery Skin and Emphysema

Older smokers often have skin that is stiff and leathery. Leathery skin and emphysema are the same thing in different tissues. The lungs, instead of being soft, supple, flexible tissue that can expand and contract as you breathe, also become stiff like old leather. People with this disease often feel heavy and can't move easily. They can't get enough oxygen from the air to do all the things we normally take for granted.

Leathery lungs don't work as they should. They can't expand and contract to get air into the small sacs, the alveoli, and get the carbon dioxide out. Consequently, when emphysema is advanced, the sufferer may even have to get about in a wheelchair. Both leathery skin and emphysema are the result of accelerated aging that comes from environmental toxins.

The protein that makes up skin consists of 22 sub-units we call amino acids. Think of a protein as a large string of beads that contains 22 different kinds arranged any way you want. You can guess there's almost an indefinite number of proteins, because your string can have ten beads, ten thousand, or more.

Imagine folding and twisting the beads to get even more variety, because you can make almost an endless structure in that way. Now think of doing it with other proteins, and you get an idea of the protein and tissue variety available in nature.

But there's a problem. Toxic chemicals we call aldehydes can react with the 'beads' and link them together. This is called cross-linking. You can cross-link within one protein or more. When all this cross-linking occurs you form a rigid structure that isn't as flexible as each string of beads. In fact it's as though the beads were taped together every so often between, across and within strands. You'd have a massive but not very flexible structure. Excessively cross-linked skin collagen is like this.

What I have just described for beads is what happens in leathery skin and, worse still, in lungs that have emphysema. The proteins – mostly collagen – have become so cross-linked that the tissue flexibility is gone. The tissue becomes thick, rigid, and loses its ability to stretch and contract. This cross linking is used in the plastics industry to convert soft plastics to stiff, hard plastic. It is not a good idea for skin and lungs.

Another problem emerges because in smokers the glands that produce fluid don't work as well. This means the skin will be coarse, because the sebaceous glands are no longer secreting oils and lubricating the dead cells of the epidermis. In the lungs, the quality of the alveolar fluid declines. This means the lungs are even less flexible and can't extract oxygen from the air as well as they should.

The best way to stop cross-linking is to trap the aldehydes. The best way to trap aldehydes is to cause them to react with vitamin E, other tocopherols, beta carotene, and all the antioxidants discussed in earlier chapters. Further, exercise helps flush them from your body.

How Much Supplementation?

I'll review a good supplement plan for smokers to assure them of enough antioxidants.

- Vitamin C: minimum 500 mg daily, preferably 2,000 (two grams) daily.
- Vitamin E: minimum 100 IU daily; preferably 400 IU daily.
- Beta carotene: minimum 25 mg daily, preferably 30 mg or more daily.
- Selenium: 75 to 150 mcg daily.
- B complex: 100 to 450 times the RNI daily.
- Mixed brassica vegetables – at least 8oz (200 g) daily.

CHAPTER ELEVEN

Pregnancy

Smoking and pregnancy don't mix. Children born to women who smoke are likely to be smaller. Sixty per cent are more likely to be born prematurely and thus develop asthma in their early years and have behavioural problems. Such children are more likely, too, to have a cleft lip and palate. We can therefore correctly say that smoking causes birth defects. The risk of birth defects and premature birth should give the prospective mother the strength to stop smoking before or at least while she's pregnant.

Being a realist, however, I know many women can't stop smoking even when they're pregnant. Women who smoke or live with a smoker and plan to have a child should take the recommendations in this chapter very seriously.

Pre-conception Nutrition

Not many years ago, if a woman thought she was pregnant, her doctor usually said, 'Come and see me after you've missed two periods.' That approach to pregnancy is as obsolete as yesterday's newspaper. Nowadays we know that preparation for pregnancy should begin three months before conception. Nutrition is preventative medicine and food is the vehicle of its practice. There is no better way of preventing problems than with pre-conception nutrition.

Birth control and our knowledge of conception has become so precise that most couples can plan the day of conception. Women should prepare their bodies to meet the challenges and demands they will experience during pregnancy. Also important, by improving their own health status and building extra protection against the effects of smoking, women give the baby a major chance of better health.

The objective of pre-conception nutrition is to build the mother's body so it will serve her and her child in the best possible way during pregnancy. If the mother breast-feeds her baby after birth, following the pre-conception nutrition plan helps make that time healthier for them both.

You've already begun if you've taken to heart the information in the previous chapter about preventing osteoporosis. You can take one of the most important steps towards a successful pregnancy by getting between 1,500 and 2,000 milligrams of calcium daily and engaging in a sensible amount of weight-bearing exercise. This combination will build – and even re-build – strong, dense bones. If you continue this calcium regimen and exercise appropriately while pregnant and nursing, you will retain this extra bone strength after the baby is born. So you'll improve your own health permanently.

Smoking and Birth Defects

Although it's not known for certain why infants born to women smokers have a low birth weight, two good theories were recently confirmed in research at the Harvard Medical School. First, smoking reduces the oxygen-carrying capacity of the blood. Haemoglobin, a protein in our red blood cells, gives the blood its red colour and carries oxygen to all our tissues. During pregnancy the mother's haemoglobin carries oxygen to the infant's blood system as well.

The carbon monoxide from smoking, living with a smoker, or even from working in a smoky environment increases the amount of carbon monoxide in the blood. Carbon monoxide, a product of combustion, attaches to the haemoglobin better than oxygen and blocks its oxygen-carrying ability. This reduces the blood's ability to carry oxygen and means that the mother and baby don't get as much oxygen as they would if the mother didn't smoke. The solution is two-fold: increase blood-borne antioxidants, which can trap carbon monoxide and spare haemoglobin, and build more haemoglobin as healthy red blood cells. In short, pregnant women should aim to increase the total oxygen-carrying capacity of the blood.

A second theory teaches that nicotine causes

tightening of blood vessels in the placenta. The placenta is the organ that develops in the womb so that nutrients can pass from the mother's blood into the infant's blood. It's an elaborate natural exchange centre where the two circulatory systems come together but do not mingle with each other. This tightening of the blood vessels is not confined to the placenta only. It's another reason that smoking contributes to high blood pressure in women, especially in the last three months of pregnancy. Obviously you can't eliminate nicotine if you choose to smoke during pregnancy. However, by following the advice in Chapter 6, and using the omega-3 oils you can help counter the nicotine-constrictive effect.

Other materials in smoke – the oxidants – destroy many nutrients. These include all the antioxidant nutrients, such as vitamins C and E, selenium, beta carotene, other carotenoids, and the special antioxidant nutrients in vegetables. A large reservoir of these antioxidants is necessary so the baby can build its protective antioxidant reservoir. These antioxidants also neutralise the oxidants in the blood, helping its oxygen-carrying capacity.

Cleft lip and palate are variations of what are called neural tube defects. The neural tube develops during the first eight weeks of pregnancy. This tube, which will be the baby's spinal cord, can't develop correctly if sufficient folic acid isn't available. As I mentioned, this B vitamin is likely to be short in average diets and especially in the diet of smokers. And smoking can destroy folic acid. The shortfall plus the destruction of folic acid add up to trouble and could explain why cleft palate and lip occur with such frequency in children born of smoking mothers. Consequently we must pay special attention to the B vitamins, especially folic acid, in pre-conception nutrition and during pregnancy.

There is even something you can do to protect your baby from developing asthma. Although we don't understand asthma prevention, we can learn from people who live in areas where asthma is rare. Their diet is rich in the same omega-3 oils that will help reduce the constrictive effects of nicotine.

Building Red Blood Cells

Red blood cells are so important that several organs in the body are well equipped to build them. Indeed, in the time required to read this paragraph your body will make about 100,000 new red blood cells, mostly in bone marrow tissue. If you can boost that natural production of blood cells by between one and three per cent, you'll be at a great advantage. Some theories say this could even reduce the likelihood of morning sickness.

During the first three months of pregnancy, your body will make an enormous amount of red blood cells to meet your increased need to carry oxygen to the baby. Hence, we know your body has the extra capacity to build these cells – it's just a matter of getting it started early.

If your diet is rich in protein, you should have a good supply of haemoglobin which will carry oxygen. But if you are short of iron, you will not have the ability to make the required amount of red blood cells.

To build haemoglobin-rich red blood cells, you've got to convince your body that you need more oxygen-carrying capacity and give it the tools to build that capacity. Therefore, you need to supply the iron needed to make haemoglobin as well as a few extra nutrients and also to start an aerobic exercise programme.

The best way of getting enough iron is to take an iron supplement daily. A good iron supplement also contains some vitamin C, which improves iron absorption. Using iron supplements along with calcium can make you constipated. Fibre and lots of water are the best combination to counter this. Eat a high-fibre cereal daily and follow the diet plan in Chapter 14. Exercise and fibre act synergistically on bowel regularity. Eat plenty of fibre-rich foods, exercise in the morning, and the chances are that you'll have regular bowel movements. This regularity will improve many body functions as well as skin tone.

Exercise and Pregnancy

Exercise is one of the best means of helping all body functions become consistent. Aerobic exercise is discussed in more detail in Chapter 13. If you're planning to become pregnant, you should definitely be healthy enough to exercise before the pregnancy. After you're pregnant, consult your doctor before beginning any exercise programme. Here I'll give you the bare bones so you'll see what you need to accomplish.

Aerobic exercise is exercise where air is required. This means exercising so you breathe hard or just on the verge of running out of breath. That rules out brisk walking and easy swimming. Instead, it calls for jogging, rapid cycling (exercise bikes are fine), skipping, fast swimming or exercise devices such as a rowing machine. Your objective is to increase your pulse rate to about 80 percent of its usual capacity, say to between 135 to 150 beats per minute, and keep it at that level for 15 minutes. Do this at least five days each week.

Start slowly. You might not be able to jog or skip for 20 minutes at first, so jog for two minutes, walk and catch your breath for one minute and slowly increase the jog times until you can do the entire 20 minutes. Your body will get the message and will at the same time put its haemoglobin building capacity into gear.

Blocking the Constrictive Effects of Nicotine

Nicotine is thought to constrict the blood vessels in the placenta. This slows the passage of nutrients from the mother's blood to the infant's blood supply. This constriction is a sort of minor starvation, causing low birth weight and limiting the level of oxygen going to each organ. Can a smoking pregnant woman do something to relax the blood vessels and counter this constrictive effect? There is no clear answer to this question. However, we do know that substances called prostaglandins control constriction and relaxation of the blood vessels. Your body produces these hormone-like substances from oils you get in food. The objective is to give your body the prostaglandin building blocks.

Your diet probably has an abundance of the omega-6 oils such as corn oil and other vegetable oils. The omega-6 oils produce the prostaglandins that tighten blood vessels. If you're typical, your diet is probably short in the omega-3 oils that your body needs to make the blood vessel-relaxing prostaglandin. You can change this balance by eating fish, using oils rich in the omega-3 oils and using omega-3 oil supplements.

By starting three months before conception, you will actually be able to alter the fat distribution in your body enough to make a difference when you become pregnant. Continue into your pregnancy and, by the third month, or six months after starting the programme, you will have achieved a good level of the omega-3 oils.

The body needs about six months to make enough of a change in its omega-3 oils to matter. This knowledge has been derived from clinical studies on people who have inflammatory diseases. Although these people start feeling results in a month, careful measurements have proven that it takes about six months to achieve the full effect.

More on Omega-3

How do you get enough omega-3 oil? One way is to eat the omega-3 rich fish described in Chapter 6. Four or five servings weekly is excellent – it's a case of 'more is better'. Linseed oil is an easy way to take omega-3 oils. A tablespoon added to your high-fibre cereal is a very convenient way of getting the best balance of omega-3 oils. Edible linseed oil can be bought in most health-food shops. It should be refrigerated. Your body converts it to the active omega-3 oils as you need them. Omega-3 oil supplements are often sold in capsules. These usually contain all three omega-3 oils.

Although clinical proof is thin, there's plenty of circumstantial evidence that the omega-3 oils will also help prevent asthma in your baby. In areas of the world where people eat a diet rich in omega-3 oils, asthma is rare.

Continue with omega-3 supplements while breast-feeding your baby, and you will get plenty of the nutrients essential to developing brain and eye tissue. Fish really is brain food, because that's one human tissue where these oils are absolutely essential. It won't hurt to give your baby a head start and improve your own health in the process.

Block the Toxic Effects of Smoking

Antioxidants are as important for the developing baby as they are for the mother. However, it's tougher for the baby to get them from the mother's blood. In order for antioxidants to transfer to the infant's blood supply, the mother must have a higher than normal supply in her own blood. This is necessary because of how nutrients and toxins transfer from the mother to the infant.

The placenta consists of myriad small blood vessels from the mother's body and from the infant. Though they don't allow blood to flow from one body to the other, they allow nutrients and toxins to pass from these small capillaries of the mother into the infant's blood. Similarly, but in reverse, toxins from metabolism in the infant's blood move into the mother's blood and are removed by her kidneys. This exchange of nutrients and toxins between mother and infant works very well. Indeed, it works so well that even cigarette smoke toxins pass easily into the baby's blood. However, they don't pass back quite so easily.

Biological membranes, such as in the placenta, allow the nutrients and toxins to pass from regions of high concentration to regions of low concentration. Because the mother does the smoking, it follows that her blood will have a higher concentration of oxidants and other by-products of smoke, including nicotine, than the baby's blood. So the toxins pass easily to the baby. Because of its immature liver, the baby's body cannot destroy the toxins. However, we can take advantage of the placental transfer system with the antioxidants and build the baby's reserve.

If the mother keeps a high blood reservoir of the known antioxidants, such as beta carotene, vitamin C, vitamin E and selenium, the baby will get a higher level from the placenta transfer. If the mother eats a diet rich in vegetables, the baby will obtain additional antioxidants as well. Although we don't know to what extent the baby can build higher levels of its own protector substances, a better diet plus supplements in the mother gives the baby the best chance. Therefore I recommend the antioxidant levels listed in Table 10.1.

Although the supplement recommendations may seem high, they aren't according to some experts, who would recommend more. You may also baulk at the extra servings of fruit and vegetables. However, these amounts will help you and the baby. All you must do is find those you like and eat them regularly.

Extra Vitamin B Complex

In Chapter 4 I discussed the B vitamins and explained how a smoker's basal metabolism is higher than average. The human need for B vitamins is directly proportional to the rate of metabolism. In this chapter I've recommended that you start an exercise programme which will increase your metabolism even more. These factors combined with our objective of building red blood cells to expand your oxygen-carrying capacity add up to a need for more B vitamins. Follow the recommendations in Chapter 4 and take a B vitamin supplement if you aren't already taking one. Remember, it is best to take all the B vitamins together.

Water

Your body calls for about four pints daily. Most of us aren't likely to drink that much water directly, but we get it from the beverages we take during the day, and also from vegetables and fruit which are about 75 to 80 per cent water.

Pregnancy imposes special demands on your excretory system. Your body must process the extra by-products that come from the foetus and from the additional processes your body is carrying out. While your kidneys process about 50 gallons of blood daily when you're not pregnant, they must process 60 to 70 gallons during pregnancy.

Water is absolutely essential for the kidneys to remove toxins from the blood and pass them out in the urine. More water is also essential so your stool will be easily moved and sufficiently hydrated. Well-hydrated stools are about 75 per cent water, which means they are especially good at removing toxins.

Drink at least eight full glasses of water daily. You should drink one glass at each meal, one when you take your supplements, and one with each table-spoon of fibre. These glasses are essential, so don't compromise.

Coffee

Although cigarettes might be impossible for you to give up during pregnancy, I urge you to drop coffee. Caffeine from coffee enters the foetus's blood, but its liver can't metabolism caffeine rapidly enough for it to clear, so it remains there for longer than it should.

No studies have evaluated the combined effect of coffee and nicotine on foetuses. However, since both are handled by the liver we can speculate that the combination demands more of the liver than either one alone. Therefore, if you've chosen to continue smoking, at least eliminate coffee. In any case, consuming plain water will help clear your body of both caffeine and nicotine.

Breast-Feeding

Most authorities nowadays are in favour of nursing a newborn baby. Mother's milk is a unique formula that contains all the nutrients and protector substances a baby needs to thrive. And the composition of mother's milk changes as the baby grows to meet its changing nutritional needs. However, environmental toxins can find their way into mother's milk. It follows that if a nursing mother smokes, the baby is getting some nicotine and other chemicals in the smoke. That can't be good for the baby. More and more experts are counselling pregnant mothers not to nurse their babies if they continue to smoke. Follow or even exceed the pre-conception nutrition plan faithfully if you continue to smoke.

Your Doctor's Advice

Your doctor will give similar advice – stop smoking during pregnancy. I sincerely hope you will follow that advice. But if you choose not to, you should certainly inform him or her that you are following the steps

I suggest in this book. Here are some of the questions a doctor might raise.

High Vitamin C Levels

Many years ago it was proposed that vitamin C at levels of one gram daily during pregnancy could cause what was tentatively called rebound scurvy. This hypothesis was based on two babies, born of mothers taking lots of vitamin C, with mild gum sores. According to this theory, during pregnancy the developing foetus becomes accustomed to high blood levels of vitamin C. After birth, the baby's blood levels return to normal, and so, the hypothesis taught, the foetus's body reacted as if it were deficient. You might think of it as a relative deficiency of vitamin C. Subsequent research has proven that this type of rebound scurvy does not occur.

My objective in building high vitamin C levels is to neutralise some of the chemicals, mainly oxidants, in tobacco. When vitamin C neutralises these chemicals the effective level of vitamin C is dramatically reduced. Because the tobacco chemicals are transferred across the placenta to the baby's blood, it is essential to continue with high levels of vitamin C throughout pregnancy.

Other Antioxidants

Vitamin E and beta carotene have been tested for safety at over 3,000 IU of vitamin E daily and 300 milligrams of beta carotene daily. That's beyond any level you'd be likely to use. These antioxidants can do much good and no harm.

Omega-3 Oils

Omega-3 oils at high levels – 16 or more grams daily – cause some changes in blood-clotting tendencies that could be harmful for people at risk from stroke and heart attack. You aren't using an extra 16 grams of omega-3 oils. You're using a level that's similar to eating an extra daily serving of salmon.

One Last Plea

After reading this chapter you might have a renewed interest in stopping smoking during pregnancy. Do it. Stop! But still go ahead with the plans I've outlined for pre-conceptual care and pregnancy. The residual effects of smoking last for about a year, so these steps will counter them. You'll be healthier for keeping to this programme, whether you've stopped smoking or not, and your baby will benefit even more than you.

CHAPTER TWELVE

Infants
and Children

A large body of scientific studies, spanning around 20 years and reviewed recently at Manchester University, shows beyond any doubt how children are affected by living with smokers. About 50 ailments in children are linked to the smoke they breathe from their parents' cigarettes.

Many conditions aggravated by passive smoke are minor. They include sore throats, irritated eyes, sneezing and coughing. But some are serious. They are meningitis, cystic fibrosis, pneumonia, cot death, asthma, some forms of heart disease and higher cancer risk later in life. Some of these conditions, such as cystic fibrosis, are congenital. While not actually caused by passive smoking, it is made significantly worse. Others, such as meningitis and pneumonia, are caused by exposure to viruses. However, children exposed to passive smoke are more susceptible to these illnesses and smoke aggravates them. Dr Anne Charlton of Manchester University showed that more cot deaths occur in smoking households. Although the cause of cot death is unknown, it's probably a case where smoke aggravates the causes. My objective here is to discuss what you as a parent can do to reduce the risk of any of these illnesses.

The best approach is either to smoke outdoors or to set aside a smoking room where your babies and children aren't allowed. This will reduce dramatically their exposure to smoke. Another positive approach to protect your children from the effects of your smoke is to start them eating the right kind of diet and taking food supplements.

No-one knows the extra nutrient and antioxidant needs of children who breathe passive smoke. It's safe to say their needs are significantly greater than average – in my opinion, possibly two or three times greater, if not more. It's important to recognise that these children will not get these levels of nutrients from their diet if they eat what the average child eats. Therefore supplements are essential. But let's start with diet first.

Chapter 14 outlines the Smoker's Longevity Diet and illustrates it with a week of menus. This plan also applies to children who live with passive smoke. Their nutrient intake will be adjusted by the amount of food they eat, so don't try and make them eat adult portions! Let them eat the amount they are comfortable with. Simply refuse to offer 'junk food' alternatives. I've never seen children starve when offered wholesome food, even if the parents have to 'wait it out'. Children will learn to like good food if they see their parents setting a good example. Most children like to please, so give them a good but realistic target to aim at. Don't worry if they want to put a little butter or ketchup on their vegetables. It may detract slightly from their health value, but if it gets them to eat it won't matter.

Supplements are different. Those made for children are usually incomplete and over-sweetened. You can get powdered or liquid ones for babies and chewable ones for toddlers and upwards. But if you look carefully you can usually find a supplement supplying all 17 nutrients listed in Table 12.1 in an acceptable form that has moderate flavouring and isn't sweetened to a fault.

Once a child is five or six years old he or she can generally swallow a complete supplement. At that age extra vitamins E and C and beta carotene are also appropriate. These will build an ongoing antioxidant reservoir that gives the child an added measure of protection. Another step is to mix a teaspoon of linseed oil in their food, such as cereal.

Note that I am giving mostly excess amounts here to the RNI, particularly when it comes to minerals. But these are my personal recommendations for children who are exposed to smoke.

Fibre is as important for children as it is for adults. Getting children to take fibre is quite easy, because they seem to like breakfast cereals and fruit. Choose a cereal that has at least four grams of fibre per serving. A child's serving topped with some fruit provides essential nutrients and gets a child off to a good 'fibre start' in the morning. You can also follow the advice given in Chapter 5 and give your child a fibre supplement. Just use about one-third to one-quarter of the adult serving size. Mix it with real fruit juice and you've added some

TABLE 12.1 *Nutrient needs for children 1–3 and 4–6 years*

Nutrient	Ages			
Vitamins	*1–3*		*4–6*	
Vitamin A	400	R.E.[1]	500	R.E.
Vitamin D	400	I.U.[2]	400	I.U.
Vitamin E	6	I.U.	7	I.U.
Vitamin C	40	mg	45	mg
Thiamin, Vitamin B_1	0.7	mg	0.9	mg
Riboflavin, B_2	0.8	mg	1.1	mg
Niacin	9	mg	12	mg
Vitamin B_6	1.0	mg	1.1	mg
Folic acid	50	mcg	75	mcg
Vitamin B_{12}	0.7	mcg	1.0	mcg
Minerals				
Calcium	800	mg	800	mg
Phosphorus	800	mg	800	mg
Magnesium	80	mg	120	mg
Iron	10	mg	10	mg
Zinc	10	mg	10	mg
Iodine	70	mcg	90	mcg
Selenium	20	mcg	20	mcg

[1] R.E. = Retinol equivalents: 2,250 micrograms beta carotene or 5,000 micrograms of carotenoids.
[2] I.U. = International Units

extra nutrients to the child's diet. It all helps meet the increased needs of children of smokers.

Give your child additional protection against a smoky

environment by ensuring he or she plays outdoors in a safe environment in fresh air. Children are naturally active, so encourage them to be active somewhere there is clean air. This exercise has the same benefits for them as it does for adults. Make sure they play out of doors regularly.

Children are natural snackers, so use this tendency to advantage. Encourage them to snack on fruit, such as apples, pears, oranges and grapes, and easily eaten vegetables such as carrot sticks and celery. Fruit and vegetable juice supply the same nutrients. There is no way children can get too much of these healthy foods, and every bit they eat helps protect them a little more form the chemicals in the smoke they're exposed to. Be wise. Encourage a healthy diet, exercise and give appropriate supplements to help your children overcome the ill effects of passive smoking.

Exercise
for Smokers

Most smokers I talk to are convinced smoking is so bad for them that it's a waste of time to exercise. Nothing is further from the truth. I believe the average smoker can benefit more from regular exercise than a non-smoker. Exercise not only counters many of the bad effects of smoking, but it will improve the physical health of a smoker just like anyone else.

While exercising, the temperature inside your muscles increases to about 102 degrees from its normal 98.6 degrees F. That 3.4 degree rise (three per cent) increases the rate of metabolism over 17 per cent, which increases circulation by at least 100 per cent. This change in circulation brings more oxygen to all the organs and tissues, including the brain, and at the same time flushes toxic wastes from your body. It's like the rain cleaning dirty streets. That's why regular exercise reduces the risk of cancer, heart disease, and just about every known disease.

Physical Exercise is Important

Every organ and tissue in your body improves if it is correctly exercised. By exercising regularly at the right level, you gain and maintain lean body mass, increase heart output and reduce blood pressure. Exercise will keep you from becoming fat and help build a reserve capacity necessary to reach your optimum potential in every aspect of life. It helps you mentally as well as physically.

Exercise increases muscle mass, improves muscular tone, and changes muscle chemistry for the better. Lean muscle has a higher basal metabolic rate (BMR) than untoned muscle, because its chemistry is different. By exercising, you increase muscle mass, thereby reducing total body fat and increasing your overall BMR.

The quality of all lean body mass is interrelated. Improved muscle tone is accompanied by better bone density, which means stronger bones and slower aging. You are also rewarded with better posture and, if you are a woman, less likelihood of osteoporosis and the shattering bone fractures that can occur in old age.

A Healthy Heart

Moderate, regular exercise improves cardiac output, reduces blood pressure and increases lean body mass. Many studies have shown that regular exercise over six or more months reduces blood pressure by about nine per cent. But this is only average – it can be much more than that, as high as 13 per cent. For some people, a nine per cent blood pressure reduction will remove them from the high blood pressure category and put them into the 'high-normal' category. With some dietary changes added to the exercise, they are home and dry.

Improved cardiac output means the heart pumps more blood with each beat. In other words, regular exercise improves the pumping efficiency of the heart. It builds your heart into a stronger muscle. You gain reserve capacity because you have more heart-output potential than you usually need.

But I must repeat: you've got to exercise regularly, and it takes time for the results to show. 'Regular' means at least five times weekly, and although the effects start to become obvious in about a month they are not really clear until about six months. After a year, there's no comparison with how you were to start.

Unexpected Benefits

Exercise is synergistic. That means its sum is greater than its parts. Put simply, if you add the benefits of exercise to your dietary programme, you will get something even greater than you would have imagined.

Satisfaction comes with accomplishment. We respond to positive reinforcement. You will begin to find mental satisfaction as you gain physical flexibility, shift fat to muscle and perform tasks you once had thought impossible. Mental alertness always improves with exercise, because improved muscle tone brings improved circulation. Improved circulation brings more oxygen and nourishment to your brain. It's not surprising that people who exercise are more alert and mentally quick.

Sleep will be sounder, not because you are tired – on the contrary, you will have more energy. You sleep better because everything about your body is more efficient. And although the restorative power of sleep remains a scientific mystery, no one can ever doubt its value, both mental and physical.

Regularity of bowel function will improve too – another of the synergistic benefits of exercise plus diet. Although dietary fibre improves regularity and bowel function, the regular exercise tones all muscles, including those of the bowel, and helps the bowel to respond easily and regularly. People who exercise regularly have better intestinal tone and are less likely to get intestinal disorders, such as diverticulosis, irritable bowel syndrome and haemorrhoids. A recent study shows that people who exercise halve their colon cancer risk.

For reasons which are not well understood, smokers have more abdominal fat. This means both men and women have a slightly higher waist-to-hip ratio. Although it seems minor, this ratio indicates a tendency to heart disease. However, this need not be a problem. You can reduce your waist-to-hip ratio by exercising. Indeed, if you follow the programmes in this chapter, you'll reverse this tendency within six to 12 months. It's one more reason why smokers can benefit more from exercise than non-smokers.

In Chapter 4 you met the vitamin B family. Your need for these vitamins is determined by your size and energy use. Exercising and smoking both increase energy expenditure, so it follows that your body will rely more on the B vitamins to stay healthy. Follow the guidelines I gave earlier so you do not fall short of these essential nutrients.

Why Exercise Regularly?

Regular exercise builds and tones the cardiovascular system, including collateral circulation, which is the development of small arteries in the muscles in and around the heart. These extra blood vessels improve your health and aerobic capacity.

When you exercise regularly, new blood capillaries start developing. It's as if your body wants to open new avenues of nourishment for your tissues, so it starts developing new channels to get oxygen-laden blood to the increased muscle mass. When you exercise regularly, you will notice that a difficult exercise becomes easy all at once. This is because the new blood channels take time to make, but then they open all at once. Think of it as a big road construction project where all the new roads open at one time. It is like that with your body. Suddenly you can do things you thought you would never achieve.

Your brain works the same way. Have you ever tried hard to learn something seemingly impossible? Then one day it was easy, like a revelation. It is the same with exercise. Only in your brain, new neuron networks open all at once, and they give you new thought patterns.

Why Exercise Does More for Smokers

Smoking puts carbon monoxide into your bloodstream. Carbon monoxide reduces the oxygen-carrying capacity of the blood by tying up haemoglobin, the protein that carried haemoglobin. A forty-a-day smoker loses about seven percent of oxygen-carrying capacity, and a sixty-a-day smoker loses ten per cent or more to carbon monoxide. It's almost that bad for people who work in poor environments. Smokers must increase their oxygen-carrying capacity by about ten per cent to stay equal to non-smokers.

Seen from another point of view, smoking reduces your physical aerobic capacity by at least ten per cent. You are taxing your lungs' ability by forcing them to deal with smoke. If you build a higher capacity than average, you can cancel out these effects and build your aerobic capacity beyond its normal levels.

You're doing what athletes accomplish by training at high altitude. At 5,000 feet the air pressure is lower than at sea level, and the cardiovascular system must work harder to obtain sufficient oxygen. When athletes train at that altitude, their bodies respond by building more capacity than normal. Then, when they compete at lower altitudes, their cardiovascular capacity is better than average and their athletic performance isn't limited by their oxygen-carrying capacity. As a smoker, you're doing the same thing by exercising regularly. Your blood will respond by building its capacity. However, your brain is sceptical and wants to be assured this programme is going to be maintained. Once convinced, it will instruct your system to go ahead and build!

Can You Do It?

No-one is so unfit, so overweight, or so handicapped that they can't exercise. I have even seen an 81-year-old woman start an exercise programme to help her arthritis. My own mother, at 85 years old, uses a stationary bicycle regularly and pedals for 10 to 20 minutes. I have seen wheelchair athletes, and I can no longer accept a physical handicap as an excuse. There's an exercise available to everyone. Similarly, there are excuses available to everyone, such as the following:

- 'But I don't have time!'
  - Nothing is as important as your health, but nothing is so easily avoided as doing something to help it. You'll just have to get up earlier, change your eating patterns, or stop work earlier. You CAN find the time out of 24 hours a day. Also, since one of the benefits of regular exercise is that you require less sleep, you'll be able to get up earlier and exercise more!
- 'It's dark and dangerous in the early morning or early evening.'

- No excuse! The range of excellent indoor exercise devices available nowadays that have been tested and proven effective makes it possible never to go outside.
- 'But I'm so out of shape and I've been smoking so long that it'll take too long for me to get in shape.'
  - Remember, it doesn't take as long to get in shape as it took to get out of shape. Furthermore, you should start slowly and work up. A good start is to walk 30 minutes at a vigorous pace each day. That doesn't even require special shoes – just ones that don't cause blisters. Work up to a 50 minute walk and you're on your way.

Stan's Story

Stan is an old friend, an astrophysicist by profession, and a smoker since the age of 18. By the age of 35 Stan was so out of shape that he would cough and wheeze whenever he had to climb a flight of stairs. His doctors, friends and relatives told him to stop smoking. He didn't. I told him to start jogging. 'But,' he said, 'I smoke. Jogging won't do me any good and may even kill me.'

'Rubbish,' I said. 'It won't kill you any sooner than it will anyone who's out of shape. Smoking is no excuse for not exercising. It'll do more good for you than it will for a non-smoker.'

I challenged Stan to meet me every morning when I jog. We didn't jog together at first because I was in shape and he wasn't. He did what he could while I did my usual course. Afterwards we'd meet again and Stan would have a smoke while we talked. About eight months after he started jogging, Stan could jog alongside me and do 2.5 miles at 7.5 minutes a mile. Yes, he still has a smoke after his daily jog, but in his own words, 'I've never felt better in my life.'

I can add that Stan has never looked better. His physical condition is good. His skin has gone from a dull 'smoker's grey' to a bright, healthy colour. He also follows all the advice in this book. So, follow Stan's example and gain a whole new lease of life!

Different Exercise Effects

Aerobics are the most efficient exercises for improving and maintaining general body fitness. Aerobic means 'air' but specifically, the oxygen in the air. Your muscles need oxygen to function, and their need for oxygen goes up dramatically when you exercise long enough. By 'long enough' I mean at least 12 minutes for very active exercises such as fast skipping, 20 minutes or longer for others such as jogging, and 40 minutes for brisk walking. All these will produce aerobic conditioning.

Regular aerobic exercise, correctly carried out, does more to tone and firm muscles than any other type of exercise. It is the most efficient way to remove muscle fat and increase muscle metabolism – and you will not get fat again if you maintain the fitness programme.

Pushing a muscle steadily for the correct time by jogging or walking leads quickly to loss of fat and good tone. Stop-and-start exercises, such as tennis, don't accomplish the same thing as quickly. Non-aerobic exercises, such as weight lifting, take a long time to remove muscle fat. Neither do they condition your heart muscles. In fact most strong weight lifters can't run a mile because the general condition of their heart and arteries is often poor. Weight lifting is called anaerobic exercise, which means 'without air.'

Aerobic vs. Anaerobic Exercises

'Anaerobic' is a slight misnomer. Actually you do still breathe when you do anaerobic exercise, but you don't exercise your heart and arteries and elevate your general metabolism. When you elevate your general metabolism, as in jogging ten to 12 minutes or more, you build your entire cardiovascular system. That's why this type of exercise is called aerobic. Your heart and arteries, indeed your entire cardiovascular system, is mostly muscle and requires exercise more than any other system in your body. By doing some form of aerobic exercise you prevent build-up of fatty deposits in your heart and arteries and can even remove some. As mentioned earlier, these deposits are the foundations of heart disease. Preventing or eliminating them through exercise is one of the most important ways you can prevent heart disease.

In contrast to anaerobic exercise, aerobic exercise

works large muscle groups, such as the arms and legs, challenging the cardiovascular system. In this way, major muscle groups and the cardiovascular system are conditioned together. Aerobic fitness produces entire body fitness.

Aerobic and anaerobic are the two extremes of exercise. Aerobic is steady exercise of long duration. Anaerobic exercise is taken in short sharp bursts. Table 13.1 classifies different exercises by type.

TABLE 13.1 *Exercises classified by aerobic content*

Aerobic (Long duration)	Stop and Go (Intermediate)	Anaerobic (Short duration)
Cross-country skiing	Badminton	Croquet
Cycling	Calisthenics	Field events
Jogging	Downhill ski	Golf
Rowing	Football	Isometrics
Running	Handball	Lawn bowling
Skipping	Racquetball	Sprinting
Stationary cycling	Tennis	Weight lifting
Trampoline-rebounder	Volleyball	
Walking (brisk)		

Aerobic exercise improves your heart rate over a period of time, if done for long enough. To achieve this, you must run for a minimum of 12 minutes or walk briskly at least 20 minutes. Anaerobic exercise such as a 100-metres sprint causes your heart to beat very rapidly, because you have created an oxygen debt by using energy from reserves without air. You breathe rapidly because your heart and lungs are trying to 'catch up' to repay the energy debt you have created while those reserves are restored. Oxygen is required to restore the reserves, so we call it an 'oxygen debt'. Weight lifting, for example, seldom causes your heart to beat very rapidly unless you create an oxygen debt, as you can do in the sprint, and it is simply catching up again. You can convert an anaerobic exercise into an aerobic one. A good example would be lifting a light weight rapidly up and down for about 20 minutes or more. But it is much better to jog, skip or swim, because these exercises are more effective and involve many muscle groups, not just one.

Tennis is stop-and-start. Unless you are very unusual, you will have to play tennis for at least two hours to get any real exercise effect. If an amateur tennis player gets a high heart rate, it is usually due to an oxygen debt. Golf I consider is a good way to ruin a healthy walk. You walk, stop, swing, talk, then walk again. Your heart never gets to even a moderately high steady beat.

Training Effect

A 'training effect' is scientific jargon for saying that you have done something that has exercised and improved your cardiovascular system. It has probably also helped you build muscles, such as those in your legs and arms, in the process. When you finish, you will be in better condition than when you started. Seems worth doing, doesn't it?

To get the full training effect, you need to:

- Achieve an elevated heart rate (see next section) quickly and do the exercise for at least 12 minutes, preferably 20 minutes.
  OR
- Achieve an increased heart rate and keep it up for at least 30 minutes and preferably one hour.
  OR
- Combine the two requirements by achieving a modestly increased heart rate and keeping it up for at least 20 minutes and preferably 40 minutes.

You should also do the exercise on five days a week. Exercise is only effective when it is done regularly and with some rest periods, such as a day off every three or four days. Once you have been using one form of exercise regularly for a year and are in shape, it is a good idea to use several forms of aerobic exercise on different days or weeks to improve. You will definitely improve, because each exercise has its own benefits.

Knowing Your Heart Rate

Become familiar with your heart and how it works. You should take your pulse while resting, while walking at a moderate pace and at a brisk pace. Try taking your pulse during a slow jog or when cycling or during a swim, stopping briefly to do so. It should be under 100 beats per minute within 10 minutes of stopping working hard, and it should slow down to normal within about 20 minutes. An easy way to take your pulse while walking or jogging is to grasp your neck gently under your jawbone with your left hand, so your thumb can feel the back of your jawbone. Press your thumb in slightly and you will feel your pulse.

For most people, a training heart rate is about 80 per cent of their maximum heart rate (maximum is the fastest rate at which your heart can beat). Some well-trained athletes will achieve the maximum during exercise under the guidance of an expert coach. But most world-class athletes train at 85 per cent of maximum. So most experts conclude that if average people get to 75 or 80 per cent of maximum, they are getting an excellent, safe training.

Table 13.2 lists maximum heart rates and 75 per cent of maximum to guide you. The last column lists the 10-second pulse rate you should aim for, so you can keep track of your progress. Multiply this 10-second rate by six to get your heart rate per minute. Once you get into a regular exercise programme, you will need to take your pulse only occasionally to make certain you are not overdoing or underdoing your exercise.

Don't worry if you can't achieve 75 per cent maximum. Some people have a lower resting heart rate. At age 57, my own resting heart rate is 54 or less (the average for my age is 72). I don't achieve 128 very easily, so I don't bother to try. I get a good training effect at about 90 percent of the average for most people. If your heart rate is low, you are already blessed with a good cardiovascular system. Strive for about 90 per cent of the training rates given in the table. For me, that's

TABLE 13.2 *Training heart rates (for average people)*

Age	Maximum	75% Maximum	10-Second Pulse
20	200	150	25
25	195	146	24
30	190	143	24
35	186	140	23
40	182	140	23
45	179	134	22
50	175	131	22
55	171	128	21
60	160	120	20
Over 65	150	113	19

about 115 to 120. You can work yours out from the chart.

But there is one rule for people who don't reach the training rate easily. We need to exercise longer in each session. The price of better-than-average health is to work a little harder to keep the gift you have.

Oxygen Debt

All exercise requires oxygen. The same basic combustion process that lets the engine of your car burn petrol is at work in your body. Both require oxygen and fuel – only in the case of your body it's glucose and fat. However, unlike your car engine, your body can go without oxygen for brief periods. But when it does so, you have to pay back the oxygen debt without delay.

A short burst of activity, such as running for a bus or climbing stairs, leaves you gasping for air and your heart beating rapidly. This happens because your body used high-energy materials to let you do that task and didn't burn your glucose all the way to carbon dioxide. It has let you create an oxygen debt.

To pay back the oxygen debt, your heart beats quickly and you breathe fast to get blood to your lungs. When your blood passes through your lungs, you get rid of the carbon dioxide and take on more oxygen. Your liver and muscles then use the oxygen to process the wastes they have built up, and you pass the carbon dioxide to the air the next time you pass blood through the lungs. No engine can duplicate this process we carry out every day with such ease. If you stop the supply of air to your car, it will simply stop running.

However, creating an oxygen debt doesn't build a good cardiovascular system. It doesn't even build a reasonable reserve for future situations, so it will not work for training.

But you can build yourself up for short-term, aerobic exercise. Have you ever noticed how sprinters run long distances to build capacity? Then they use short-distance sprints to build their muscles and timing for the sprint. But their capacity comes from aerobic training. They build their anaerobic technique onto an aerobic foundation. Doing this correctly requires an expert coach.

The Best Way For You

The best exercise for you is, simply, the one you will do regularly, consistently, and long enough to achieve a training effect. Look over table 13.3 to help pick the exercise you like best. It lists three groups of aerobic exercise according to the approximate time required to develop a good training effect. In each category I have listed the sort of time it takes to achieve a training heart rate and then the time for a conditioning effect. Less vigorous exercise requires a longer time.

TABLE 13.3 *Typical aerobic exercises*

Group 1 1–1.5 min. to THR* (12 min. minimum)	Group 2 3 min to THR (30 min. good time)	Group 3 8 min. to THR (50 min. good time)
Bench step	Aerobic dancing	Brisk walk
Jumping jacks	Cross-country	Cycling
Running on the spot	skiing	Skating
Skipping	Jogging	Swimming
	Rebounder	
	Rowing	

*Training heart rate.

You can modify most of these exercises to meet your own needs. Let's go through each group to discuss its qualities.

- Group 1 consists of exercises for people who are already in good condition. These are borderline anaerobic exercises that can be done long enough to get a training effect. If you haven't been exercising, you are likely to develop sore muscles from doing them. It is also difficult to exceed the 12-minute minimum due to boredom and staying in one place. Exercises in the other two groups are easier.

- Group 2 exercises can be done by anyone who is reasonably healthy. Some exercises, such as jogging and aerobics, can be done in organised groups. Others, such as cross-country skiing and rowing, involve the use of equipment. The rebounder or mini-trampoline is a device that works well in a small room. Even jogging can be done on a machine at home or the gym.

- Group 3 exercises are the best starting point for everyone. These exercises can be done either alone or with others. I recommend you start with 20 minutes and work up to 50 minutes or more. This may seem like a long time, but that is what it takes to get your cardiovascular system working at the right level. It's not always easy regaining health. No pain, no gain!

Exercise Equipment

Almost every aerobic, outdoor exercise can be duplicated at home. You can even watch television while cycling, jogging, rowing or cross-country skiing on machines. Technology has made it possible for everyone to become physically fit without leaving the house. A few rules apply:

- Never use motorised devices. The motor is doing the work, not you.
- You get what you pay for. Studies have shown that the most effective devices are more expensive.
- Simple is better. The best devices just require you to use your arms and legs actively. You don't need added heart monitors and other electronic gadgets.

Which exercise machine is the best? This is a matter of personal preference, although I rank them in the following order:

- Cross-country skiing machines. These exercise the arms and legs independently. You work all the major muscles and don't 'pound' your joints.
- Stationary bicycles. These require you to use your arms and legs at the same time. They develop resistance as the wheel turns. The only minor flaw is that the arm and leg exercise is linked together. Therefore they are not quite as good as cross-country skiing because one exercise powers the other and the total effort is divided between the two.
- Stationary joggers, treadmills. These are excellent for the legs and can simulate hills and be as difficult as you need. The only drawback is that your arms are generally inactive. In fact they are less active than if you actually jogged.
- Rowing machines. These can be excellent if you have an independent arrangement for leg exercise with a movable seat. Most of them exercise the upper body very well. If they have a moving seat, the legs get good exercise as well. If you have leg trouble, you

can't beat these machines because you can exercise the upper body alone.

Aerobics Classes

Some people like to exercise in a group or under the guidance of an instructor. Aerobics, or aerobic dancing, is the thing for them. It requires a leader who sets the pace according to the fitness and physical limitations of the group. 'Low impact' aerobics are good for people who are just starting, or have joint problems or are overweight. When you are advanced enough, you can do aerobics wearing hand and foot weights to burn extra calories and strengthen muscles. There's an aerobics level for everyone.

Stretch and Tone

Every aerobic exercise programme should include about 15 minutes of stretching and toning. These are exercises that require you to stretch the tendons in your arms and legs. They should also force you to exercise muscles in hard-to-reach places. They can be as simple or as elaborate as you want them to be. You should always do a few basics. Do each one ten times at first, working up to 30 daily.

- Situps. With knees bent, situps help to strengthen and tone abdominal muscles. Put your arms behind your head and try to reach your knees with your elbows.

- Leg raises. Lying on your back, raise one leg to a 90 degree angle, hold it for a second, and put it down. Lie on each side and raise the leg as high as you can (it probably won't be very high). This tones muscles inside the thighs and helps reduce fat.
- Hip rotation. This is done standing with legs apart. Touch each leg in turn with the opposite hand, and come up straight after each.
- Stretch. Stand straight, cross your legs, and touch your toes in one sweeping motion starting with your hands together high over your head. Then cross your legs the other way and repeat. This helps stretch leg tendons and keeps them from getting stiff.

Video Workouts

There's no substitute for having an expert instructor. Television can bring one into your home. If you own a video you can buy or hire aerobics or stretch and tone tapes for any level you require. They also enable you to take the time to learn each exercise correctly and progress at your own, comfortable pace.

When to Start

This moment is the beginning of the rest of your life – so now is a good time to start. By the time you finish reading this paragraph you will have 100,000 new blood cells and about 14,000,000 other cells. They need the extra air! If you haven't been exercising, start slowly.

A brisk 40-minute walk is an excellent way. Then progress to brisk walking for five minutes, followed by a one-minute jog then five minutes of walking, and continue in this manner for 40 minutes. A healthy person with no leg or heart problems should be able to maintain a 12–15 minute per mile pace for 40 minutes – that's two and a half to three miles. A practised brisk walker will do a mile in ten minutes. Experiment with different forms of aerobic exercise to find the one that suits you and your lifestyle.

When to Exercise

Most exercise programmes fail because of bad timing. Modern lifestyles are so complicated that both discipline and experimentation are necessary to find out what is best for you. Some people find they can get up early in the morning and get their exercise over and done with for the day. Others use their lunch breaks for jogging or doing exercises. Some find it more effective to come home from work and start exercising then. This can be a good way of removing the tensions of the day. There really is no 'best' time, only the one that suits you.

Exercise not only tones the body, it relieves stress and relaxes the mind. Most people feel the highest level of stress at the end of the day, so exercise helps the mind then as much as the muscles. However, early morning exercise provides a different advantage. Whenever you exercise, your brain produces natural opiates called endorphins, which lift your mood so you feel more positive. While they help you feel better at the end of the day, they also help you start the day with an optimistic outlook. So while the evening is biologically a little better for exercise to relieve stress, morning exercise gets you off to a good psychological start.

Studies have shown that people who exercise in the morning are less likely to give up, because most people have more control over the early part of the day before other obligations take over. Morning exercisers also find they are more efficient during the day. So for many people, the morning is the best time. But there is no reason not to exercise. All you have to do is find the best time for you, and get started.

Will I Be Tired?

No! People who exercise gain more stamina. Stamina is staying power – the energy to keep going for hours. Every study has proven that people who exercise regularly increase their stamina by large measure over people who don't exercise. Look at it this way. Exercise makes your body and mind more efficient. Your metabolism is higher, but your heart works less to maintain the system. Your blood sugar doesn't fluctuate, so your moods remain at an even level. It all adds up to being more effective.

A conditioned body also seems to create an optimistic outlook. I think it could be due to the natural endorphins at work and also the confidence that comes from accomplishment. Whether you are a business executive, a secretary, a housewife or an athlete the results are the same – condition your body and you condition your mind. People who treat their body with love and respect have more confidence in themselves, and they radiate this to their fellow human beings.

Start now!

CHAPTER FOURTEEN

Smoker's Longevity Diet

The Smoker's Longevity Diet puts all the nutritional information I've given you into everyday practice. It's a balanced diet by all the accepted criteria for good health.

If you follow this diet and use all the supplements I described, I promise that within a week you will feel better than you have for a long time. You'll sleep more soundly at night and get up with more bounce in the morning. Within a month you'll look better – and people will notice. Stick with the diet plan and your risks of cancer and heart disease will decline.

Other more minor but important benefits will accrue. Your skin won't wrinkle as quickly. You'll recover from ailments faster. you'll have more energy and be more mentally alert. And if you're overweight, you'll drop the extra pounds. Add exercise, and you'll convert body fat to muscle. You'll be pleased with the 'new you'.

Many people live to eat. I want you to learn to eat to live. The Smoker's Longevity Diet is endless in its variety. No two meals or snacks ever have to be the same. Once you work this diet into your lifestyle, it will become a habit – the best habit you'll ever develop!

Protective Eating

Fruit and Vegetables: 7 Servings Daily

Determine serving size by comparing with the following examples.

Vegetables: 4 oz/100g cooked or 8 oz/200g raw
Examples: 1 large stalk broccoli with the floret; 6 medium asparagus spears; 2 potatoes without skin or 1 baked potato with skin; 1 medium raw carrot.

Fruit: 1 medium apple, orange, pear, etc; 3 small plums or apricots; ⅛ large cantaloupe; ½ small melon; 1-inch slice watermelon.

Five Rules Apply

- Eat one serving of a cruciferous vegetable daily.
- Eat one serving of deep green or dark red vegetables, such as spinach, broccoli, sweet red pepper, carrots daily.
- Eat one serving of fruit raw, such as an orange, apple, or banana, daily.
- Eat three servings of beans, such as butter beans, red kidney beans, lentils, weekly. Change varieties regularly.
- Eat one serving of a mixed salad with tomatoes and onions daily.

Grains and Cereals: 4 Servings Daily

Determine serving size by comparing with the following examples.

Cereals: ⅓ cup cold or cooked; use cereals that provide

4 or more grams of fibre per serving.
Breads: 1 slice wholegrain bread or 1 wholegrain roll.
Pasta: 1 cup cooked (2 ounces dry).
Grains: ½ cup cooked.

- Eat one daily serving of a high-fibre, natural cereal with low-fat or non-fat milk. Try to eat three varieties of high-fibre cereals weekly.

Natural Bulbs: I Serving Daily

Serving size is variable. The following objectives apply: Eat garlic, onions, leeks, shallots, and chives regularly. Examples: Use 1 clove of garlic to flavour a salad, soup, meat, spaghetti sauce, etc.; ¼ onion in your salad or with some vegetables; ¼ cup chopped raw leeks. Flavour foods with these bulbs regularly. You can't eat too many bulbs.

Milk and Dairy Products: 3 Low-fat Servings Daily

Determine serving size by comparing with the following examples.
Milk: ½ pint
Yoghurt: 6 ounces
Cheese: About 1½ ounces

- Although ice cream is a dairy product, one full pint is needed to fulfil the nutritional need. Frozen yoghurt is somewhat better, because it contains fewer calories, but it still calls for 1 pint. Newer low-fat ice creams are better yet.

Protein-rich Foods: 2 Servings Daily

Determine serving size by comparing with the following examples.

Fish, fowl (white meat): 3½ ounces (about ¼ pound)
Eggs: 2 medium
Cheese: 1½ ounces
Beans: 1 cup cooked

Weekly Rules to Follow

- Eat fish at least four times; fresh at least three times.
- Eat one vegetarian meal; for example, pasta with cheese; eggs; beans.
- Eat fowl, such as chicken, turkey, or duck, as often as desired; remove the skin after cooking.
- Eat red meat only once weekly; never is better.
- Don't eat processed meats, such as burgers, hot dogs, and the like.
- Eat visible eggs (e.g. scrambled, poached) a maximum of two eggs three times weekly.

Oils and Fats

The best oils for:
Frying: are peanut oil or butter.
Baking: are canola or rapeseed oil.
Salads: are olive, canola, walnut, avocado, and linseed.

- Add 1 teaspoon corn oil to salad dressing and in baking to increase your intake of the omega-3 oils.

Water

- Drink four 8-ounce glasses daily. Use purified water, mineral water, or distilled water.
- Seek out water that is free of nitrates, chlorides, and man-made chemicals, such as pesticides. Water rich in natural minerals, including calcium and magnesium, is best.

I encourage you to go beyond the diet and include more fish and poultry and less red meat, also more vegetables and fruit. Develop some habits which I'm sure you've heard before, but which are worth repeating:

- Always eat fruit for dessert instead of puddings or ice cream.
- Snack on cut-up vegetables, fruits and nuts instead of chocolate, sweets and buns.
- Always use wholewheat bakery products instead of white breads.
- Drink a half pint of water first thing in the morning, 30 minutes before you eat, and once before bedtime.

Supplementation

If you follow the Smoker's Longevity Diet, you'll be getting plenty of fibre, carotenoids, bioflavonoids, folic acid and other nutrients that protect your health. However, as a smoker you need extra fibre and higher levels of many nutrients, especially vitamins B complex, C and E and the carotenoids. So, do you need to take supplements?

I think that in this day and age, sensible dietary supplementation can help everyone – especially smokers. They are not a substitute for a good diet, but they will make it even better. Diet will always be the foundation for health, but supplementing it provides even greater efficiency. Even though there is some controversy amongst scientists and nutritionists about whether you can get all you need from the so-called 'balanced diet', I believe that supplements are like an additional insurance policy. Estimates show that less than ten per cent of us eat in a balanced way.

Stress in our modern world imposes far greater nutrient demands on our bodies than food alone provides. Even if you follow the Smoker's Longevity Diet, you're never going to have enough vitamin C or E, or omega-3 oils. You are also likely to fall short of fibre, calcium, copper, zinc, vitamin A and folic acid. These shortfalls can be made up by using supplements, but the supplements won't make up for the food. The bottom line is: you need both. Assess your own diet against the Smoker's Longevity Diet and what you've read in this book to see where your own shortfalls are.

A brief word about general nutritional recommendations. In 1991 the Committee on Medical Aspects of Food Policy (COMA) decided on certain dietary requirements and intakes, and these have been the ones referred to in the general recommendations throughout this book. I believe, though, that certain nutrients are required at a higher level than the RNI (recommended nutritional intake). One example is vitamins C and E. The higher level is needed because they don't just serve as vitamins, but also as protectors. They neutralise toxins, and each one is destroyed in the process. That's why the 'protector function' is not always the same as the 'vitamin function'. For the same reason, we also need more protective beta carotene than is required to make vitamin A.

If you exceed the RNIs by taking even up to ten times the amounts specified for most vitamins, you will have no toxicity symptoms – with two exceptions. They are vitamins A and D. Don't confuse beta carotene or other carotenoids with vitamin A. Beta carotene is converted to vitamin A in the body only as required. You can't get toxic levels of vitamin D from sunshine because your body has the built-in safety of its skin pigments. But serious abuse of vitamin A and vitamin D supplements creates a toxic situation. Use common sense.

Beyond the Basics

I believe that smokers and people who live with smokers need even greater supplementation than the recommended nutritional guidelines and basic supplements suggest. My own suggestions are:

Vitamin C
If you take 500 to 2,000 mg (2 grams) daily, you will have a sufficient excess to cover all eventualities. Be sure the supplement you take contains bioflavonoids.

Vitamin E
Research supports about 100 IU of vitamin E daily for

average people, and 400 IU for smokers. So I think it makes sense to take a vitamin E supplement.

Beta Carotene

I would like to see a supplement that contains a mixture of carotenoids, such as lycopene, and others. But failing that, I urge you to take 25 mg of beta carotene daily. In addition to that, snack on tomatoes, carrots, and other red and yellow fruit.

Calcium

Make sure you get 1,000 mg of calcium daily and up to 2,000 mg if you're past the menopause. You can do this with extra dairy products or calcium-magnesium (always together) supplements.

B Complex

The most basic reason for a smoker to take extra B complex vitamins is elevated metabolic rate, but there are other reasons. For instance, they are necessary if you're under a lot of emotional or physical stress, or take drugs such as birth control pills or high blood pressure tablets. I think in these cases you can take as much as four or five times the RNI of these nutrients. Choose a complete B-complex vitamin supplement that is balanced with all the B vitamins.

Fish Oil

Even if your diet is excellent, you can still benefit by taking extra fish oil – up to 1,000 mg daily. Alternatively, or at the same time, you can put a tablespoon of linseed oil on your cereal or in a salad each day with the dressing.

Garlic
Garlic supplements have been available for a long time. I'm not convinced that they are as effective as eating fresh garlic, but they ensure an high intake if you are not keen on eating it as part of your diet.

A Waste of Money?

Many people worry about spending money on supplements, but consider what else you spend money on: beer and wine, biscuits and cakes, coffee and tea, soft drinks – and of course, cigarettes. I'm not telling you to stop spending money on the things you enjoy, but I want to convince you that spending on something positive for your health is not a waste of money.

Megadoses – Are They the Answer?

Megavitamin users often think that vitamin supplements can make up for not eating a good diet. They get pleasure from food, and seek nutrition from pills, thinking that they can eat anything as long as they take copious quantities of supplements. This is not how it works. Nutrition is far from being an exact science, even today. You still need a balanced food intake as well as supplements. For instance, certain factors in food, such as flavonoids, seem to make vitamin C more effective or can replace it altogether. Similarly, there are about 350 other carotenoids in foods besides beta carotene. The roles of these are not well understood, but they are important. Therefore, if your diet isn't up to scratch you will miss out in a way that no supplement can make up for.

High doses of nutritional supplements may be helpful, however, in cases of serious health problems. Here you would be best to consult a nutritional advisor.

Slow Changes

You are unlikely to notice significant changes overnight even when you start the diet and supplementation. Improving your nutrition pays powerful dividends, but they accumulate slowly.

An aggressive programme of self-help includes diet, lifestyle and supplementation. If you want to see how well this plan works, you should keep a personal health diary for a month or two, in which you record how you look, feel, sleep and wake up. You won't be disappointed, because you'll see results. A diary is the best way to get in touch with your body and understand your feelings, and discover what to do for the best 'you'.

To give some examples, people who follow a diet plan to lower their blood pressure usually detect significant results in a week or ten days. In four to eight weeks, many can stop using medication. In contrast, when people follow a diet to help arthritis, they usually get some results in ten days, mild results in about three or four weeks, but it requires six months for the obvious improvements in mobility, inflammation and pain to occur.

Similarly, smokers following the Smoker's Longevity Diet and taking supplements will be able to identify subtle but definite results within a few days, even though this is a lifetime commitment. For example, in a week or two fingernails usually become a little stronger with a healthy pink colour beneath the nail bed. This reflects better metabolism and circulation. People also notice within a few days that they sleep more soundly and wake up with more energy. In about a week, stamina improves and they feel more relaxed while having as much energy at the end of the day as at the beginning. Bowel regularity is another change everyone experiences from the start. Your bowel movements will become more frequent and regular.

These changes are indications of better general health. They accumulate so slowly that most people are unaware of them. If you stop your nutritional programme, the benefits will decline as slowly as they started. Remember, your health evolved to its present state over many years and is the sum total of heredity, environment, diet, lifestyle and emotions. The fact that you can notice an effect from diet within a few weeks is really spectacular. It shows how your body responds to a little nutritional support.

Sample Menus

Here is a seven-day diet plan that illustrates the versatility of the diet programme. The idea is to stimulate your own creativity.

Note: In the sample menus, the numbers in parentheses indicate the calorie count for specific foods.

Serving sizes:

Beverages (milk, juice, etc.); 6 ounces juice, 8 ounces milk

Yoghurt: 8 ounces

Cereal: ½ cup serving

Fruit: a medium piece, such as an apple, or a banana

Vegetables: ½ cup cooked

Bread and rolls: 1 slice or 1 roll

If sugar is added to coffee, tea, etc.: 1 teaspoon = 15 calories. (I recommend not adding sugar or artificial sweeteners, but if a sweetener is used, I recommend natural sugar.)

Sample Menus for a Week

DAY 1

Meal	*Calories*
Breakfast	
Glass of water	0
½ grapefruit	39
All-Bran cereal (50) with low-fat milk (104), ½ sliced banana (52)	206
One slice wholegrain bread (61), toasted and buttered (36)	97
Tea or coffee, optional	0
Midmorning Snack	
Glass of water; coffee or tea	0
Peach yoghurt	260
Carrot sticks	31
Lunch	
Glass of water	0

Bean soup	157
1 wholewheat roll (72) with butter (36)	108
Lettuce salad (4) with tomatoes (12), cucumber (4), green pepper (5), and onions (4), Italian dressing (14)	43
Steamed broccoli	12
Lime sherbet	135
Tea or coffee (optional)	0
Afternoon Snack	
Glass of water	0
Apple (81) with cheddar cheese (114)	195
Dinner	
Glass of water	0
Broiled salmon with herbs	100
Baked potato (88) with sour cream and chives (26)	114
Steamed broccoli	12
Salad (see lunch)	43
Low-fat ice cream (140) with sliced strawberries (22)	162
Tea or coffee, optional	0
Evening Snack	
Pear	98
Day 1 Total	**1,812**

DAY 2

Breakfast

Glass of water	0
8 ounces orange juice (fresh squeezed)	111
Slice of cantaloupe	57
Oatmeal (109) with raisins (56), low-fat milk (104)	169
Wholewheat muffin (170), butter (36)	206
Tea or coffee, optional	0
Midmorning Snack	
Glass of water	0
Bran muffin	112

Lunch

Glass of water	0
Tuna fish salad (172) sandwich on wholewheat bread (140)	212
Carrot sticks	31
Coleslaw	42
Tea or coffee (optional)	0

Afternoon Snack

Glass of water	0
Pear (98) with feta cheese (75)	173

Dinner

Glass of water	0
Cheese ravioli with tomato sauce with onions, garlic, spices	284
Mixed salad greens (5) with tomatoes (12), green pepper (5), garbanzo beans (32), Italian dressing (14)	68
Dish of spinach	6
Cannoli	171
Tea or coffee, optional	0

Evening Snack

Apple	81
Total Day 2	**1,723**

DAY 3

Breakfast

Glass of water	0
Orange-grapefruit juice	80
Sliced oranges and strawberries	55
Wholewheat waffles (206) with maple syrup (50)	256
Tea or coffee, optional	0

Midmorning Snack

Glass of water	0
Cheddar cheese (114) and grapes (75)	189

Lunch

Glass of water	0
Salmon quiche	215
Triple-bean salad	90
Pear	98
Tea or coffee (optional)	0

Afternoon Snack

Glass of water	0
Carrot and celery sticks	35

Dinner

Glass of water	0
Stir-fried chicken with broccoli, red peppers, onion, garlic, ginger, and mushrooms	266
Rice	112
Mixed green salad (5) with water chestnuts (15), green onions (7), and mandarin oranges (23), Thousand Island dressing (24)	74
Apple-tapioca pudding	101
Tea or coffee, optional	0

Evening Snack

Banana	105

Total Day 3	**1,676**

DAY 4

Breakfast

Glass of water	0
Slice of melon (57) with blueberries (41)	98
2 poached eggs (158) on wholewheat toast (62)	221
1 slice lean ham	50
Tea or coffee, optional	0

Midmorning Snack

Glass of water	0
Blueberry muffin	176

Lunch

Glass of water	0

Curried chicken salad on lettuce	136
Banana bread	85
Frozen banana yoghurt	143
Tea or coffee (optional)	0
Afternoon Snack	
Glass of water	0
Grapes	58
Dinner	
Glass of water	0
Halibut steak, broiled	119
Mixed green salad (5) with tomatoes (12), onions (7), red pepper (6), zesty tomato dressing (11)	38
Carrots	31
Asparagus	12
Rice	112
Apple strudel	96
Tea or coffee, optional	0
Evening Snack	
Piece cheese (105) and wholewheat crackers (70)	175
Pear	98
Total Day 4	**1,648**

DAY 5

Breakfast	
Glass of water	0
Sliced oranges, bananas, and kiwi fruit	72
Fibre cereal (60) with low-fat milk (104)	164
Bran muffin (112), butter (36)	148
Tea or coffee, optional	0
Midmorning Snack	
Glass of water	0
Fruit yoghurt	260
Lunch	
Glass of water	0

Lentil soup	69
Melted cheese and crab on English muffin	238
Mixed salad greens (5) with tomato (12) and cucumbers (4), zesty tomato dressing (11)	32
Brussels sprouts	30
Pear	98
Tea or coffee (optional)	0

Afternoon Snack

Glass of water	0
Celery sticks (12) with peanut butter (47)	59
Carrot sticks	31

Dinner

Glass of water	0
Courgette lasagne with tomato sauce with onions, garlic, and herbs	189
Corn	89
Lemon, cabbage, carrot terrine with lettuce	57
Crusty French bread, butter	81
Cheesecake	150
Tea or coffee, optional	0

Evening Snack

Plum	36

Total Day 5	**1,803**

DAY 6

Breakfast

Glass of water	0
8 ounces orange juice (fresh squeezed)	111
½ papaya	59
Fibre cereal (60) with low-fat milk (104) and blueberries (41)	205
Tea or coffee, optional	0

Midmorning Snack

Glass of water	0

Fruit yoghurt	260
Lunch	
Glass of water	0
Spinach salad with mushrooms, chopped egg, onion, bacon bits; oil, vinegar, and mustard dressing	218
Broiled salsify	46
Popover	90
Sliced peaches	66
Tea or coffee (optional)	0
Afternoon Snack	
Glass of water	0
Rice cakes (35) with cream cheese (98)	133
Dinner	
Glass of water	0
Fillet of sole	80
Basil bean salad with onions, garlic	90
Rice pilaf	121
Spinach	6
Pumpkin pie	212
Tea or coffee, optional	0
Evening Snack	
Pear	98
Dried apricots	83
Total Day 6	**1,878**

DAY 7

Breakfast	
Glass of water	0
Sliced peaches (37) with low-fat cottage cheese (41)	78
Wholewheat pancakes (142) with blueberries (41) and maple syrup (50)	233
Tea or coffee, optional	0
Midmorning Snack	
Glass of water	0

Fruit yoghurt	260
Dried apricots	83
Lunch	
Glass of water	0
Creamy carrot soup	149
Salmon salad with lettuce and tomato in pita bread	136
Raspberries	61
Tea or coffee (optional)	0
Afternoon Snack	
Glass of water	0
Apple muesli bar	134
Dinner	
Glass of water	0
Marinated lamb roast with garlic	180
Tossed greens (5) with sliced canned pears (50)	55
Small roasted potatoes	65
Green beans	22
Broccoli	23
Wholewheat roll with butter	70
Lemon dream parfaits	176
Tea or coffee	0
Evening Snack	
Orange	65
Total Day 7	**1,790**

Calories Count

As you look over the menu plan, you'll notice that each food item has its approximate calorie count and the daily calories are totalled to prove that you won't get fat eating this way. In fact, if you're overweight now, and you start living by the Smoker's Longevity Diet, your weight will slowly drop to normal.

However, this isn't a weight-loss plan. It's a healthful, sensible way of eating. Any weight loss comes because you're eating a more bulky diet with less fat and less sugar. You'll feel full and won't get cravings.

Index